THE KIDNAPPING OF JOURNALISTS

RISJ CHALLENGES

CHALLENGES present findings, analysis, and recommendations from Oxford's Reuters Institute for the Study of Journalism. The Institute is dedicated to the rigorous, international comparative study of journalism, in all its forms and on all continents. CHALLENGES muster evidence and research to take forward an important argument, beyond the mere expression of opinions. Each text is carefully reviewed by an editorial committee, drawing where necessary on the advice of leading experts in the relevant fields. CHALLENGES remain, however, the work of authors writing in their individual capacities, not a collective expression of views from the Institute.

EDITORIAL COMMITTEE

THE KIDNAPPING OF JOURNALISTS

REPORTING FROM HIGH-RISK CONFLICT ZONES

ROBERT G. PICARD AND
HANNAH STORM

REUTERS
INSTITUTE for the
STUDY of
JOURNALISM

Published by I.B.Tauris & Co. Ltd in association with
the Reuters Institute for the Study of Journalism, University of Oxford

Published in 2016 by
I.B.Tauris & Co. Ltd
London • New York
www.ibtauris.com

ISBN: 978 1 78453 589 6
eISBN: 978 0 85772 859 3
ePDF: 978 0 85772 842 5

A full CIP record for this book is available from the British Library
A full CIP record is available from the Library of Congress

Library of Congress Catalog Card Number: available

Typeset by Riverside Publishing Solutions, Salisbury, SP4 6NQ
Printed and bound in Great Britain by T.J. International, Padstow, Cornwall

MIX
Paper from
responsible sources
FSC® C013056

Contents

List of Illustrations

About the Authors

Robert G. Picard is North American Representative for the Reuters Institute in the Department of Politics and International Relations at the University of Oxford and a fellow of the Royal Society of Arts. He was formerly Director of Research at the Institute and a research fellow at Green Templeton College (Oxford). He is the author and editor of 30 books and has been editor of two leading journals. He received his PhD from the University of Missouri, Columbia, and has been a fellow at the Shorenstein Center at the John F. Kennedy School of Government at Harvard University. He has consulted and carried out assignments for governments in North America, Europe, Africa, and Asia and for international organisations including the European Commission, UNESCO, and the World Intellectual Property Organization. He has been a consultant for leading media companies in North America, Europe, Asia, Africa, and Latin America.

Hannah Storm is Director of the International News Safety Institute (INSI), which provides safety advice and training to journalists working in dangerous situations. Its members include the BBC, CNN, and Al Jazeera. Before joining the INSI in 2010, Storm spent more than a decade working as a journalist in television and radio, and online for outlets including the BBC, *The Times,* and ITN. She started her career as a graduate trainee at Reuters after reading English at Oxford University. She is the author of *No Woman's Land: On the Frontlines with Female Reporters,* which explores the unique safety issues of women who work in the media. She also works as a freelance consultant for different UN agencies with a specific focus on gender and media.

1

Journalists are Vulnerable Targets

The practice of journalism is increasingly dangerous and attacks on journalists continue unabated. A particularly troublesome feature of this violence is that a rising number of journalists are being kidnapped for ransom or held as hostages. This growing global problem threatens the practice of journalism and the ability of news media to fully inform the public about events occurring in the world.

Journalists and media workers are highly vulnerable to kidnappings because they often work in dangerous locations, seek access to adversaries involved in conflicts, and may have to rely on shadowy contacts and sources in carrying out their work. Just how vulnerable journalists are in kidnap scenarios was starkly illustrated by the executions of James Foley, Steven Sotloff, and Kenji Goto by Islamic militants in 2014 and 2015. Their killings represented an escalation of the price paid by journalists and news organisations trying to cover developments in locations of crisis and conflict around the world.

This book explores the challenges faced by news organisations in attempting to protect journalists, in responding to kidnappings of their journalists, and in covering abductions of one of their own. It explores the familial, governmental, and economic influences on news organisations during kidnappings and lays out some good practices for avoiding, preparing for, and responding to the horror of a kidnapping. The intent of this volume is to increase the understanding of the environment in which kidnappings and their responses occur, the issues they pose, and the challenges that the journalism community encounters as it responds to these abductions. This publication attempts to improve journalists' and news executives' understanding by exploring what happens when news organisations and other parties involved must react to the kidnapping of journalists.

The capture and detention of journalists in conflict zones by combatants has long been an unwelcome consequence of pursuing stories

1

during wars and conflicts. These detentions sometimes result in assaults on journalists, but the journalists are typically released within a relatively short time. In recent decades, however, there has been an increase in the number of journalists kidnapped for exploitation as hostages or for ransom. These are highly worrisome because these kidnappings sometimes continue for years, result in the deliberate killings of journalists, and tend to halt – or at the very least hinder – on-the-ground coverage of regions where they occur by reducing the willingness and ability of news organisations to send reporters to the areas.

Kidnapping of journalists itself is not a new phenomenon and has been a concern for decades, but a sharp rise in the number of kidnappings and the deliberate killing of hostage journalists have made the phenomenon particularly significant today. The kidnapping issue first gained considerable attention with the widespread kidnapping of Western journalists covering Lebanon in the late 1980s and early 1990s, with the captivity of the Associated Press's Terry Anderson, the *Guardian*'s David Hirst, and ABC News's Charles Glass. Later conflicts in Arab countries led to kidnappings including that of the *Wall Street Journal* reporter Daniel Pearl, who was detained and beheaded in Pakistan in 2002, and *Christian Science Monitor* reporter Jill Carroll, who was held for two months in Iraq in 2006.

Western journalists, however, are not the only kidnap targets, though they tend to get higher international media coverage. Hundreds of others from around the world have been held, attacked, taken hostage, and killed in the Middle East, Latin America, and Asia. In 2014 alone, 119 professional journalists and eight citizen journalists were kidnapped (up from 87 in 2013), according to Reporters Sans Frontières, an organisation that tracks abuses against journalists. Ukraine, Libya, Syria, Iraq, and Mexico were the locations for most of the abductions and 90 per cent involved domestic reporters while only 10 per cent involved foreign reporters.[1]

The kidnappings are one part of the increasing overall violence against journalists worldwide. Almost 1,500 journalists and news media workers died in the course of their work between 2004 and 2014, according to a recent report by the International News Safety Institute.[2] More than 800 were killed in locations not caught up in warfare, and the majority were local journalists working in countries where the absence of a rule of law, the pervasive presence of corrupt gangs, officials, and business people, and an almost over-riding impunity gives a green light to those who wish to silence journalists. The attacks are designed to threaten and intimidate those who seek to bear witness and hold the powerful to account in nations where the development of independent local journalism is now challenging the power of authoritarian leaders and economic elites.

Journalists are jeopardised when they work, travel, or live in locations in which civil authority is absent, rule of law is lacking, or human rights are disregarded. Because of the journalistic principles of bearing witness to events and seeking multiple views of conflicts, many journalists travelling and working in high-risk conflict zones seek out differing perspectives, which may offend opposing parties. In addition, the nature of their work may mean they need to seek assistance in getting to hard-to-reach locations to understand developments and gain interviews with figures in conflicts. Sometimes the only way to do this is to put their trust in and work with mysterious and unknown figures whose motives are not always clear.

These issues put journalists in perilous positions. Their presence is often unwelcome. They may be perceived as aligned with opponents and, in some cases, they are suspected of being spies. This view is often incorrect, but also viable, because security services of many states have used journalism as a cover for their agents.

Although this book is concerned with the kidnapping of journalists for ransom or as hostages, some of the safety and organisational issues involved also appear in other types of capture and killing of journalists, so it is important to understand how they differ and why broad safety training and preparation of different potential organisational responses are necessary.

One type of capture involves journalists detained or imprisoned by combatants in conflict zones. These sometimes result in assaults on and injuries to journalists, but typically do not involve holding journalists hostage for ransom or other purposes. In most cases this type of captivity involves journalists being seized and interrogated by combatants, but they tend to be released within a relatively short time period once their identities are established or outside pressures are applied to obtain their release. Examples of this type of seizure include:

- A group of journalists from CBS News, BuzzFeed and Sky News were detained as they travelled to the Ukrainian city of Slavyansk in early 2014. The group was stopped by militants at a checkpoint, blindfolded, and then interrogated during their ordeal; one of the CBS crew members was beaten.

- *Guardian* journalist Ghaith Abdul-Ahad was detained in the Libyan town of Sabratha in February 2011 by the country's army. Brazilian journalist Andrei Netto of *O Estado de Sao Paulo* was detained with him, but released on 10 March. Abdul-Ahad was released on 16 March, after the Turkish government stepped in and *Guardian* editor Alan Rusbridger flew to Libya to help win his release.
- Swedish journalists Johan Persson and Martin Schibbye were imprisoned in Ethiopia for more than 400 days after they were charged and found guilty of entering the country illegally and supporting a rebel group because of their contacts with the Ogaden National Liberation Front. The journalists maintained that they were only doing their job and trying to investigate the activities of a Swedish oil company active in the region.

This type of capture is often given significant attention by news safety organisations and gains prominent news coverage in order to pressure the combatants involved to release the journalists. The challenges created by such detentions were among the precipitating reasons for the creation of training programmes for journalists entering conflict zones and have led many large international news organisations to establish protective internal policies related to the deployment of personnel in conflict zones.

Another related phenomenon is the deliberate abduction and killing of journalists by groups and individuals to silence specific media workers or to stop their coverage. In these cases perpetrators do not make demands for their safe release, but use the killings as a warning to other journalists. These types of kidnappings include:

- The body of Mexican journalist Jorge Torres Palacios was found in June 2014 four days after he was kidnapped near his home in Acapulco. A journalist for 20 years, he wrote a regular column in *El Dictamen*, often exposing police abuses and corruption.
- French journalists Ghislaine Dupont and Claude Verlon were kidnapped and killed in Mali in November 2013 after interviewing a leader of a separatist group in Kidal for Radio France Internationale.
- Ayham Mostafa Ghazzoul, a journalist for the Syrian Center for Media and Freedom of Expression, died in 2010 under torture after being

detained four days earlier along with his colleagues who documented human rights abused by the Assad regime.

This type of danger is most often found in nations where high levels of lawlessness exist or where governments choose not to – or cannot – act against perpetrators. Journalists and news organisations have tended to respond to such killings with condemnation, provision of safety training for journalists entering these environments, or by reducing news coverage.

A third category of attacks on reporters in combat zones occurs when journalists are killed in crossfire or as the result of genuine mistakes or wilful indifference by combatants. Examples of this type of journalistic casualty include:

- Germain Kennedy Mumbere Muliwavyo from Radio Télévision Muungano, who was shot and killed in February 2014 in Oïcha, Democratic Republic of the Congo. He had been riding in a Congolese military vehicle with a number of other journalists when it was attacked by a rebel group operating in the eastern part of the country.
- Mayada Ashraf, a journalist for *Al-Dustour*, was shot and killed in Cairo, Egypt, in March 2014, while covering clashes between security forces and the Muslim Brotherhood protesters in eastern Cairo's Ain Shams area.

News organisations and journalists can do little to prevent such attacks, but can be trained to avoid or mitigate such risks or deploy only in areas where the risks for such dangers are lower.

The fourth type of danger for journalists in regions of conflict – kidnapping for ransom or hostage – differs from the three previous types of attacks because it presents a range of challenges well beyond those of the other types of attacks. Journalists in cases of kidnapping for ransom and hostage have been deliberately targeted or become kidnap victims after they were detained by combatants in conflict zones. The growing use of journalists as hostages to pressure their governments and to obtain ransoms is creating significant safety challenges and leading to a reduction of insightful coverage of developments in regions in which they occur.

The most dangerous countries for journalists, 2004–14

1. Iraq
2. Philippines
3. Pakistan
4. Mexico
5. India
6. Somalia
7. Syria
8. Iran
9. Brazil
10. Russia

Source: International News Safety Institute

Growing concern in news organisations and governments

The problems of harassment, injury, and death of journalists in areas of conflict, the capture of reporters, the deliberate killing of media workers, and the holding of journalists for ransom have spawned efforts by organisations such as the Committee to Protect Journalists, Reporters Sans Frontières, the International News Safety Institute, and other media, governmental, and non-governmental organisations to bring attention to the need to protect journalists and to help them better understand how to improve their safety during hazardous and potentially hazardous reporting activities.

Most news organisations, however, do not have crisis management plans in place to respond to the kidnapping of their journalists and lack capabilities to respond to them. These deficiencies make it very hard for media organisations initially to respond to abductions. Larger, international news organisations often have basic plans in place, but little ability to rapidly recover kidnapped journalists. 'You have protocols in place for death but with a kidnapping you don't hold too many of the cards', says the Associated Press's Sandy MacIntyre.[3] Preparation helps reduce the alarm, confusion, and organisational inertia that can be generated when a kidnapping occurs.

The rising dangers faced by journalists globally is leading to greater levels of concern and support for efforts to improve their safety and to hold accountable those who endanger, harm, hold, or kill journalists. Two significant actions calling attention to the issues occurred in 2015 involving the United Nations and news publishers. The UN Security Council passed a resolution calling for the protection of journalists in areas of armed conflict, the release of journalists held hostage, and urging governments to act against those who attack journalists.[4] Concurrently, the Board of the World Association of Newspapers and News Publishers (WAN-IFRA) passed a resolution urging governments, international institutions, and the media industry to make journalists' safety a priority and denounced the impunity surrounding the killing of journalists in many locations.[5]

Bringing the issues to the attention of governments and gaining public recognition of the responsibilities of these authorities to protect journalists has been a slow process. Responding to pressure from journalism organisations, the United Nations Educational, Scientific, and Cultural Organization (UNESCO) has spearheaded a campaign for the past decade to promote safety and counteract the issue of impunity with a plan of action for the UN as a whole. It argues that

> Most abuses against media professionals remain uninvestigated and unpunished. This impunity perpetuates the cycle of violence against journalists, media workers and citizen journalists. The resulting self-censorship deprives society of information and further impacts press freedom. The killing of journalists and its impunity directly impacts the United Nations' human rights based efforts to promote peace, security, and sustainable development.[6]

The UNESCO effort received backing from the UN Chief Executives Board and Executive Board in 2012 and 2013 and an action plan for the safety of journalists was discussed by the UN Security Council in 2013. In late 2013, the UN General Assembly passed a resolution on safety and impunity, calling on governments to protect journalists and to bring those who attack journalists to justice.[7]

Despite this attention, the attacks on and the capturing of journalists continue unabated and news organisations increasingly have to prepare for the possibility of abduction of reporters and media personnel working for them. Although each kidnapping is unique, takes place under varying circumstances, and involves groups with different backgrounds and motives, each presents some common issues to the media organisations and the journalists involved.

These kidnappings tend to take place in locations with weak governments that do not fully control their territory and occur in the midst of international or domestic armed conflicts. Because of these characteristics, waves of journalistic kidnapping and hostage taking have tended to take place as varying countries and regions have been plunged into conflict and warfare. Kidnappings also take place in countries with domestic instability caused by struggles with violent political or crime groups. In Mexico, for example, drug cartels are engaged in an ongoing conflict with the government that has claimed more than 100,000 lives since 2006, including about 60 journalists. Continuing conflict between authorities and criminal gangs in Brazil has led to attacks on government facilities, *de facto* control of some communities by gangs, and attacks on and kidnapping of journalists.

Because of the locations and parties involved, the abilities of news organisations, journalist associations, and public authorities to respond and deal with the abductions are often limited. Most news organisations remain ill-prepared to handle kidnappings of their personnel, cope with the emotional turmoil created by such abductions, and to expend the time and money required in seeking their release. Kidnappings of journalists force managers of media organisations into responses to situations in which lives are at risk, in environments full of ambiguities and complexities, with uncertain outcomes, and pressures from families, loved ones, and governments.

Those who have experienced abductions of their staff talk of the high levels of anxiety they create, how the kidnappings become an all-consuming focus of activities, and the emotional toll they take on everyone involved. 'It is a nightmare like no other you can ever go through,' says GlobalPost President/CEO Philip Balboni, who dealt with the capture of James Foley by forces loyal to Colonel Gaddafi in Libya during the 2011 uprising and then his kidnapping in Syria in 2012 that ended in his beheading in 2014.[8]

There is no way to fully prepare an organisation or its managers for the stress of a kidnapping, but knowledge about the issues and processes involved in a kidnap response and preparation of contingency plans can reduce uncertainty about how to respond, guide actions, and inform responses should the terror of a kidnapping occur.

Why are journalists kidnapped?

The kidnapping of journalists can be either premeditated or opportunistic. Premeditated kidnappings most often occur for the purpose of killing and silencing specific journalists, but sometimes are undertaken to hold journalists hostage or for ransom.

Most kidnappings in which journalists are held hostage are opportunistic because the immediate circumstances surrounding their capture make it possible. In some cases the journalists may be detained by combatants and then passed on to other groups so that the initial act of capture can transform into a hostage or ransom kidnapping. Journalists are kidnapped for a variety of reasons, but the primary reasons are to obtain ransoms, to use them in propaganda by the captors, to put pressure on governments of the journalists' home countries to change policies, or because captors believe them to be spies or apologists for their enemies.

The motives for kidnappings can change over time because kidnappers may alter their purposes or demands, because continued confinement places burdens on those holding captives, or because kidnapped journalists may be traded to other organisations in the conflict with different motives. This trading of journalist hostages among combatant groups and tribes has been a particular feature in the Levant since the start of the Arab uprising because some groups are better prepared to hold hostages or they view them as trophies for gaining a reputation among other combatants.[9] A journalist might be captured by a smaller independent combatant group which trades him or her to a larger group for weapons or money. This problem has been a significant feature in Syria and Iraq in recent years and makes it more difficult for hostage recovery teams to determine who is holding the journalist and what their interests might be.

The demands of kidnappers range from money, to release of prisoners, to national apologies and changes in government policies. These demands can change over time, complicating any negotiations for release.

Regardless of the motive of the hostage takers, journalists are available and attractive targets because their capture will be noticed and the media platforms of their employers have the potential to carry kidnappers' political views, making journalists high-value hostages if media blackouts are not employed.

The kidnapping of journalists raises significant questions about the practice of journalism in high-risk areas and about the responsibilities of employers to their journalists, whether full employees or freelancers.

In the past, for example, many news organisations have provided training, special equipment, and support for their employees but not freelancers. Some would employ freelancers to provide coverage in areas in which they would not deploy their own employees for safety reasons. This has changed more recently with several major news organisations, such as Agence France-Presse and the *Sunday Times*, publicly stating that they will not accept non-commissioned material from freelancers for fear that doing so would attract greater risk-taking. However, the stakes are high for competitive news and for every organisation prepared to follow AFP and the *Sunday Times*, there are others who are less scrupulous. Many have had freelance journalists working on the frontlines of battlefields and in dangerous locations where other media are less willing to assign reporters.

The increased hazards, however, are forcing even many aggressive young news enterprises to take measures to protect both employees and freelancers, and freelancers themselves are increasingly expecting support from those commissioning their work in dangerous settings. This situation is significantly different from the past when the dangers were lower. It is notable that signatories of the Global Safety Principles and Practices in 2015 were primarily legacy news enterprises and journalism organisations, but also included rising digital news providers such as Vice News, Mashable, and Round Earth Media.

The kidnapping of news workers also raises ethical questions for the industry because journalists and news media generally appear to be more willing to cover the kidnappings of one of their own than the kidnappings of non-journalists, partly because of self-interest and because of the effects of publicity efforts by journalist safety organisations. There are also allegations from journalists that news organisations are more willing to be silent about the kidnappings of journalists when asked to do so than they are regarding kidnappings of other persons. Whether journalists deserve more coverage and special treatment compared to other individuals because of the democratic functions served by media is debated by journalists and social observers.

Suspicion of journalists

A significant challenge for journalists in conflict zones is that some combatants or sides in the conflict may believe journalists are propagandists or spies for their enemies.

When the Associated Press journalist Terry Anderson was taken captive in Lebanon in 1985 by Hezbollah, he was accused of being a spy and held until 1991. After his release he understandably became a vocal critic of government use of journalists to obtain information and the deployment of actual spies using journalist covers. Nevertheless, those practices continue despite being long condemned by journalists' associations as putting journalists at risk.

Being a well-informed and multilingual reporter can also be problematic. After Peter Theo Curtis was captured in Syria in 2012, his hostage takers believed him to be a CIA agent and tortured him because he was knowledgeable about the Middle East and Islam and fluent in Arabic, French, German, and Russian.[10]

Suspicions that journalists are spies are not completely unwarranted. The US Central Intelligence Agency's recruitment of journalists or placing of agents undercover as journalists was purportedly banned in 1977, but CIA director John Deutch in 1996 said that the agency had a waiver that gave it the right to continue to do so.[11] A BBC investigation in 2013 revealed British journalists at the *Observer*, the *Sunday Times*, the *Telegraph*, the *Daily Mail*, and the BBC collaborated with that country's secret intelligence agency MI6 during the Cold War.[12]

The practice appears widespread and continuing. In 2006 it was revealed that the German Federal Intelligence Service (BND) used and paid at least 20 journalists working abroad as part-time spies in the late 1990s and first years of the twenty-first century.[13] Canadian journalist Mark Bourrie resigned from China's Xinhua service after being asked for information of interest to China's intelligence agencies and wrote about the problem in *Ottawa Magazine* in 2013.[14] A review of Soviet intelligence activities showed that they recruited journalists for their access, insights, and confidential information.[15]

The practice of using journalists as spies or for such intelligence gathering or using journalist covers thus increases the vulnerability of all journalists in hostile zones.

Responses to kidnappings involve multiple interests

When journalists are kidnapped, a number of stakeholders with differing interests become involved, including the hostage's employers, family, the government of the journalist's home country or countries, insurance firms, and recovery teams.

News organisations that employ a journalist or have a freelance contract with a kidnapped journalist become involved because of moral and legal responsibilities to care for personnel in the field. Kidnappers often see them as points of contact and sources of ransom, as they are likely to have greater resources than the journalist or the family of the journalist.

The families of kidnapped journalists are likely to experience great uncertainty and stress about the potential outcomes. Understandably, not least because of their close emotional involvement, they typically are asked not to play the central role in investigations and negotiations because those require a level of detachment to be effective. Sometimes choices are made to withhold some information from family members to protect them from further emotional pressure during the process. Nevertheless, families tend to be informed partners in the response process and often make the riskiest decisions when private recovery efforts take place, but they tend to be less involved when government security agencies are involved in the recovery.

The governments of kidnapped journalists' home countries become involved to varying degrees, but this can become complicated when journalists hold passports from more than one country as dual citizens. US government agencies, particularly the State Department and FBI, have traditionally liaised with and briefed families and media companies involved, but often to a minimal degree. Although government officials exhibit concern and sympathy and share their assessments, they typically do not become deeply involved in recovery efforts and have been criticised for using contacts with families and their advisers to gain intelligence that can be employed in other ways – such as to plan attacks on hostage takers that may not be in the best interest of the hostage. Continental European governments have tended to be more involved when their citizens are kidnapped because they have historically been more open to negotiations and payments on the behalf of their citizens than the US or UK, even though they ostensibly reject ransom payments – a factor that will be explored later in this publication.

When a kidnapping takes place, providers of kidnapping and ransom (K&R) insurance play a significant role in the response if the journalist's employers are covered. Most media companies do not disclose they have K&R insurance if they do because it can lead to demands for higher ransoms or encourage copy-cat scenarios.

Most insurance companies keep a low profile during kidnappings. They typically have arrangements in place with security consultants and turn over the case to them when a kidnapping occurs. These consultants investigate, make recommendations about how to proceed, and carry out agreed courses of action to try to recover kidnap victims. These consultancy firms are typically staffed by former intelligence and military special operations personnel. They tend to directly bill the insurance firm for services or can be hired by media firms without insurance or by family members of kidnapped journalists.

Balancing the interests of these parties requires significant managerial attention to create an effective response team and determine the best reactions to a journalist's kidnapping. It is a process that is not discussed much publicly, but is growing in importance and application as journalists are increasingly targeted by combatants.

In the coming chapters, this book will discuss the uneasy and sometimes adversarial relationships between those trying to recover kidnapped journalists and the governments of the countries from which the journalist derives. It will explore how employers and industry organisations respond to kidnappings, what scope of action the organisations have, the efforts they make to recover victims, and what they are doing to avoid future kidnappings. It develops lessons from the experiences of journalists, their families and loved ones, and media organisations during kidnappings and reveals the influence of external pressures on media firms from different groups, including relatives and insurance and recovery firms. It will investigate whether the news media cover journalistic kidnappings similarly or differently from the kidnappings of other individuals or groups of individuals under similar conditions and why. It discusses the roles of journalist safety organisations before and during kidnappings and lays out good practice suggestions for employers who need to respond to journalist kidnappings, as well as for other news organisations covering them.

Kidnappings involve journalists and media organisations globally, including many from regions where organisational resources and support for journalists in the field are more limited and local professional associations that can train and advocate for them are absent or less robust. The perspectives of this book are, admittedly, skewed towards established, wealthier media organisations operating from the Northern Hemisphere, particularly Europe and North America. This is not to diminish the global scope of the kidnapping challenge or its toll on journalists elsewhere, but reflects the asymmetrical roles of media and journalism associations in developed countries in producing, organising, and utilising resources, training, and recommendations for addressing the challenges posed by kidnappings. News organisations and journalists worldwide can learn from and adapt practices from their experiences and responses.

2

Relations with Governments during Kidnappings

Responding to kidnappings of journalists requires news organisations and the families of those journalists to engage with the governments of the abducted person's home countries. Tensions and disagreements often appear because of differing interests. Whilst the families and employers place the greatest emphasis on the return of kidnapped journalists, governments balance recovering the journalists against issues of foreign policy, terrorism policy, and the interests of security agencies. This regularly creates frustration, complaints, and family pleas to governments to provide greater assistance or pursue actions they do not wish to take. The challenge is heightened because hostage takers are increasingly using captive journalists in efforts to pressure foreign governments to change policies, release captives linked to the kidnappers that are held by governments, or make ransom payments on behalf of their captive citizens.

Governments around the world differ in their policies regarding how they deal with kidnap negotiations and ransoms involving journalists and other parties. In some cases governments take the lead in trying to free their citizens, but others refuse to and make it difficult for private parties to do so on their own.

US government agencies, particularly the State Department and FBI, have traditionally liaised with and briefed families and media companies of hostages. Although these agencies may exhibit concern and sympathy and share their assessments of the situation and kidnappers, they typically avoid becoming too involved and often use their relations with media and families to gain intelligence they can use in other ways. Some European governments have been more involved when their citizens are kidnapped because they have been more open to negotiations and payments than the US or UK.[1] 'Whenever terrorists kidnap a hostage, the relevant national government faces an impossible dilemma. Should they pay a ransom and risk encouraging other abductions, or refuse concessions and place the life of the captive in jeopardy?' an article in the *Telegraph* noted.[2]

The thorny issue of these disparate approaches was underscored by the killing of the American journalists James Foley and Steven Sotloff in 2014, which happened several months after the release of French colleagues who had been held alongside them. The US government had refused to negotiate with their captors and, along with the UK, had taken the lead during the previous few years in calling for the banning of ransom payments to proscribed groups.

In 2013, the major group of countries that form the G8 agreed not to pay ransoms to terrorists. The following January, this agreement was given more weight when the UN Security Council passed Resolution 2133, which called on member states to prevent terrorists from benefitting 'directly or indirectly from ransom payments or from political concessions'.[3] Even so, in April of the same year, four French journalists were released by their captors. Didier François, Nicolas Hénin, Edouard Elias, and Pierre Torres were found by Turkish soldiers blindfolded and handcuffed on the Syrian border. They were held at the same time and by the same captors as James Foley and Steven Sotloff. President François Hollande later denied that the French government had paid a ransom for the men's release. However, he did say that negotiations with their kidnappers had been going on for several weeks. Despite his denial, media reports later surfaced that contradicted his claim, stating that millions appeared to have been paid to secure the release of the men.[4]

Extract from G8 policy communiqué: Kidnapping for ransom by terrorists (18 June 2013: https://www.gov.uk/government/publications/g8-summit-kidnapping-for-ransom-by-terrorists-extract-of-communique)

The international community has made significant progress in combating the flow of funds to terrorist organisations. However, in the last three years, we estimate that Al Qaeda-affiliated and other Islamist extremist groups worldwide have collected tens of millions of dollars in ransoms. Payments to terrorists from Sahel to the Horn of Africa helped fuel instability in the region, and contributed to large scale attacks like In Amenas. The payment of ransoms to terrorist groups is one of the sources of income which supports their recruitment efforts, strengthens their operational capability to organise and carry out terrorist attacks, and incentivises future incidents of kidnapping for ransom, thereby increasing the risks to our nationals.

We are committed to protecting the lives of our nationals and reducing terrorist groups' access to the funding that allows them to survive and thrive in accordance with relevant international conventions. We unequivocally reject the payment of ransoms to terrorists in line with the UN Security Council Resolution 1904 (2009) which requires that Member States prevent the payment of ransoms, directly or indirectly, to terrorists designated under the UN Al Qaeda sanctions regime through the freezing of funds and other assets.

We welcome efforts to prevent kidnapping and to secure the safe release of hostages without ransom payments, such as those recommended by the GCTF [Global Counterterrorism Forum], specifically in the Algiers Memorandum on Good Practices on Preventing and Denying the Benefits of Kidnapping for Ransom by Terrorists. We encourage further expert discussion, including at the Roma Lyon group, to deepen our understanding of this problem. We also encourage private sector partners, including aid and media organisations, travel and insurance companies, and other businesses to adopt their own similar guidelines and good practices for preventing and responding to terrorist kidnaps.

We continue to support efforts to reduce terrorist groups' access to funding and financial services through the ongoing work of the FATF [Financial Action Task Force] to improve anti-money laundering and terrorist financing frameworks worldwide. We call on all countries to effectively implement the revised FATF Standards. But when the worst happens, we agree to provide mutual assistance to States responding to terrorist kidnaps including, as appropriate and feasible, through information sharing and specialist expertise or assistance, or the provision of resources related to hostage rescue. We will also support capacity-building initiatives to help states prevent, and prepare to respond to future terrorist kidnaps including through bringing terrorists to justice more effectively and ensuing that they do not avoid responsibility.

We call on discussions at the UN on new mechanisms to increase international awareness of the threat of kidnapping for ransom, and propose consideration of further UN Security Council resolutions to address and mitigate the threat.

We strongly support efforts by the international community to tackle other forms of kidnapping and to reduce the threat of piracy.

Less than six months later, Foley was murdered by Islamic State militants. Steven Sotloff was murdered shortly thereafter. Foley's kidnapping had been subjected to a media blackout since he was kidnapped in 2012. Media blackouts occur when information is withheld from the public and sometimes other members of the media during the course of a kidnapping. The issue of blackouts will be discussed further at a later point in this book.

Because of the blackout, none but those closest to him and a few news outlets which were contacted and agreed to keep quiet about his situation knew that he was being held by the same group who had been holding the French men and others from various countries. The US government refused to negotiate with Foley's kidnappers, but staged a failed rescue attempt. In this case and in others, France has never officially confirmed ransom payments and yet in December 2014, French national Serge Lazarevic became the country's sixteenth captive to be released since 2010. News reports at the time suggested that his release highlighted the French policy of secret negotiations to free hostages and the payment of ransoms.[5] Other countries are widely believed to have paid ransoms in order to secure the release of their own nationals who were held alongside Foley and Sotloff. In early 2015, fellow American hostage Kayla Mueller was killed in a US attack after being held by the same group. In addition to these three American captives, various Islamic militant groups were believed to have held more than 20 other hostages of Danish, German, Spanish, and Italian nationalities – many of them journalists – at the same time. However, they were released between February 2014 when French media workers were set free and February 2015 when news emerged of Mueller's death.

At the time of writing, British photojournalist John Cantlie, who was kidnapped alongside Foley, is still believed to be held, and his situation appears to be complicated by the refusal of the UK government to negotiate and pay ransoms.

The fact that some hostages were released and others killed highlights the legal and ethical dilemmas faced by those governments whose citizens have been kidnapped and the difficulties that this in turn means for hostages and their families in instances where country policies differ. Speaking about this dilemma, journalist David Rohde, who was kidnapped by the Taliban in 2008 in Afghanistan and later escaped, has said: 'Some European governments do pay ransoms, but if you are American and you're kidnapped there is very little your government is going to do to help you, that much is clear.'[6]

While the UK and US governments have held fast to their commitment not to negotiate and not to pay ransoms, the European countries mentioned above appear to have found ways to channel funds to proscribed organisations, resulting in the release of hostages from their countries. The result of these concessions seems to be stark evidence of the fact that negotiations and ransoms result in release, whereas their non-payment does not.

Nicolas Hénin, who was released six months before Foley was killed, told the BBC: 'Being an American he was probably more targeted by the kidnappers. Well, he would be beaten a bit more probably, he was some kind of scapegoat. . . . Some countries like America but also like the UK do not negotiate and, well, they put their people at risk.'[7]

However, in turn, those nations which are believed to have paid ransoms have been accused of funding terrorism. In a July 2014 article, the *New York Times* reported that: 'While European governments deny paying ransoms, an investigation by the *New York Times* found that Al Qaeda and its direct affiliates have taken in at least $125 million in revenue from kidnappings since 2008, of which $66 million was paid just last year.' According to its investigation, the bulk of that $125 million came from European governments 'which funnelled the money through a network of proxies, sometimes masking it as development aid', adding that, 'put more bluntly, Europe has become an inadvertent underwriter of Al Qaeda.'[8]

There are arguments made for both sides regarding ransoms.

The payment of ransoms may increase the likelihood of a hostage being released, but it also increases the likelihood of more hostages being taken, particularly of the same nationality where their governments have already guaranteed a return for the kidnappers.[9] However, it also raises the price tag of other hostages, thus inflating the already immense pressures on the families, colleagues, and loved ones of those who are taken captive as nationals of non-paying countries. The burden of having to raise a ransom is left to them and they are faced with the dilemma of having to obtain more money than they otherwise might have, had other countries not paid up previously while their own country outlaws the practice.[10] In the case of the US, families, companies, or private organisations which paid ransoms could stand accused by the US Department of Justice of funding terrorism and face prosecution under regulations in place at that time, but since amended by the Obama administration.

The family of James Foley was threatened with prosecution should they try to pay his ransom. Speaking after his death, his mother Diane Foley said she was not necessarily surprised by this, but what did shock her was the manner in which the US authorities delivered the message. 'I was surprised there was so little compassion,' Mrs Foley told ABC News in September 2014 of the three warnings she had been given by US officials about the illegality of paying a ransom to the Islamic State terrorist group. 'It just made me realize that these people talking to us had no idea what it was like to be the family of someone abducted ... I'm sure [the US official] didn't mean it the way he said it, but we were between a rock and a hard place. We were told we could do nothing ... meanwhile our son was being beaten and tortured every day.'[11]

In light of this criticism and similar ones from the families of others who have been killed and kidnapped, the US government began looking again at its policies regarding support to families whose relatives are kidnapped, as well as diplomatic security and coordination. A review was launched in late 2014 by the White House and a multi-agency review team compiled a series of recommendations based on extensive discussions with a range of parties, including families. These included creating a single point of contact for family members to guide their way through what can be an extremely complicated and bureaucratic process, and to help provide better access to information for them, including declassification of intelligence. In addition, the recommendations included better access to services for families such as counselling, travel assistance, and financial management support. If the worst happens and a hostage is killed, the recommendations were to put in place a system to coordinate the death certificate and the body being returned. The Obama administration also considered the creation of a fusion cell to bring together different agencies such as law enforcement, intelligence, and other officials to allow for a more coordinated response to overseas hostage situations where US citizens are involved. Although it was suggested by some involved that the review would likely lead to the government no longer prosecuting or threatening to prosecute families who pay ransoms, this was not entirely clear during the review.

In June 2015, the US government announced that it was lifting the threat of prosecution for families communicating with and paying ransom to captors. Although it did not seek a change in the law that made it illegal to provide money or other support to terrorist organisations, the US government said it would not prosecute those who paid ransoms.[12] The review also led to the creation of mechanisms for better family engagement, the creation of a hostage recovery fusion cell and hostage response group, the appointment of a special envoy for hostage affairs, and other efforts to improve the government response to hostage takings.[13]

As previously noted, the British government refuses to pay ransoms or negotiate with terrorists. It made moves to strengthen its position in late 2014 when Home Secretary Theresa May announced that UK-based insurance firms would be banned from paying out on claims linked to ransom payments for proscribed organisations.[14]

However, in practice, it seemed that little changed with this announcement, because the funding of proscribed organisations, including through ransom payments, was already illegal. Writing in the *International Business Times* in 2014, Shane Croucher said there was a 'perceived grey area when it comes to insurance firms paying out on claims when someone has paid a ransom to a terrorist group in order to buy the release of a kidnapped person'. He quoted Tom Keatinge of the Royal United Services Institute as saying that, although the UK's position was very clear, the uncertainty could come from the fact that, because London is such a major insurance hub, insurance coverage might be provided from London to cover the payment of a ransom that originated in a country without the same tight policies as the UK.[15]

The kidnap and ransom market does not pay the ransoms. It reimburses such payments where people and groups have taken out insurance.

Documentary film-maker Sean Langan was kidnapped by a group connected with the Taliban in 2008 when he was making a film for Channel 4. He was released after the company apparently paid a £150,000 ransom for him. He says he remembers how troubled he was during his captivity by thoughts about the possible price that would be paid for his freedom that might in turn find its way into the coffers of terrorists. 'While negotiations were going on, I suddenly thought I really don't want my life and my freedom bought at the expense of the lives of innocent women and children,' he stated in a BBC article in December 2014, adding: 'I didn't want that money spent on terrorism.'[16]

As in the case of Langan, there have been other incidences where payments have been made to captors by individuals and companies. This was the case when Somali pirates were reportedly paid more than £600,000 for the release of Paul and Rachel Chandler, kidnapped from their boat during a sailing trip.

Both the US and the UK have been behind attempts to rescue hostages. However, successful attempts have been overshadowed by those that failed. In the case of James Foley, US special forces staged an attempt a month before he was killed, his identity only coming to light after the rescue mission was unsuccessful.

In December 2014, the British-born American photojournalist Luke Somers was killed alongside South African teacher Pierre Korkie during a failed attempt to rescue them from Al Qaeda's Yemen affiliate. US President Barack Obama had ordered the mission, in which ten Al Qaeda operatives were also killed, saying he believed Somers's life was in 'imminent danger' after the group posted a video threatening to kill Somers.[17] Media reports after the ill-fated mission claimed that American special forces had not even known that Korkie was being held alongside Somers. A charity that had been supporting Korkie's family reported that he had been due to be released just days later; however, the South African government said that this was just a rumour.

In 2009, *New York Times* journalist Stephen Farrell was kidnapped by the Taliban along with an Afghan colleague, Sultan Munadi. The two men had been investigating the deaths of civilians in a NATO airstrike when they were taken hostage. Talks to free them were taking place when US and UK forces launched a rescue attempt. Mr Munadi was killed along with a British soldier. His father, Kurban Mohammed, said his son had phoned him an hour and a half earlier to say he would soon be home.[18]

What is clear from the positions different governments take is that the payment of a ransom is a very complex and controversial issue and an ethical dilemma facing many countries.

The ransom issue and other policy concerns complicate the efforts of news organisations and families trying to gain the release of journalists held hostage and as such require a great deal of attention and governmental interaction during the process.

3

Organisational Responses to Kidnappings

Media organisations' responses to kidnappings depend upon multiple factors, but among the most important are whether they have prepared for potential kidnappings, have crisis plans in place, and have kidnap and ransom insurance policies. The existence or otherwise of the latter is particularly significant because it tends to direct how the response will be organised.

If an organisation is unprepared for the possibility of one of its journalists or media workers being kidnapped and does not have contingency plans in place, it will complicate and slow the response to the kidnapping, perhaps further endangering the captive individual or individuals.

Because kidnappings occur for different reasons, the planning and responses of news organisations may need to be different for kidnappings undertaken for publicity by terrorists and others, those done by criminals solely desiring ransom, and those involving efforts to intimidate and silence journalists and news organisations.

Preparation and contingency planning

News organisations sending journalists to conflict zones or contracting with freelance journalists to cover those zones need to consider and prepare beforehand for all possible safety risks, including kidnapping. They should ensure that the journalists they deploy and their editors are adequately trained to prevent injury, death, or kidnapping and that there is a contingency plan for kidnappings in place. The plan should provide the basic outline of how the organisation will organise its response, who in the organisation will be responsible for the response, what resources will be available, and what basic strategies it will employ.

Knowledge that a contingency plan exists should be available throughout the organisation, although the full plan may be available to fewer people. The reason for making contingency planning known is that relatively junior staff may become the first to be aware of an incident, and without knowledge of the plan may broadcast, print, or disseminate information to the public and colleagues in ways that may harm the response, or may be exposed to material that is potentially traumatising to them and requires an organisational response. They will need to know of an easily accessible resource that provides them with clear directions of whom to contact and what to do or not do.

The broader contingency plans need to lay out the organisation's strategy – that is, its guiding principles for dealing with kidnappings, how the response will be organised, who will be responsible for the response, and how it can be quickly implemented even by people who were not part of the original contingency planning.

Kidnap and ransom insurance

Some news organisations have kidnap and ransom (K&R) insurance, an extremely specialised form of insurance that is confidential, politically sensitive, and usually underwritten offshore, mainly in locations such as Guernsey, Jersey, or Bermuda, but with headquarters and offices in many nations (a selected list of insurance firms is found in Appendix 3). When a company has such insurance, the type of coverage and how it is accessed become part of the contingency planning and response.

K&R insurance involves two types of insurance: one involving the costs associated with responses to a kidnapping and another for the payment of ransom. The two can be bought separately, but are usually bought together. The main reason for this is that a primary motivation of the company purchasing K&R insurance may be financial: it does not want the company's operating statement and balance sheet affected by the expenses that are incurred in responding to a kidnapping and it wants to ensure it has the resources, financial and otherwise, to respond appropriately.

Kidnap insurance typically covers unlimited consultancy, which can be extremely expensive if kidnappings become long and drawn out and there is no insurance in place. Consultancy involves activities such as gathering information about the kidnapping and perpetrators and the provision of advice on dealing with kidnappers and their demands. Consultancy expenses are typically paid directly by the insurer. Ransom insurance, however, is usually a reimbursement policy, which means the insurer does not put up money for any ransom payment. Instead, the holders of such a policy have to find the money and only then will the policy pay them back for ransom payments and certain associated costs. Because it also provides a finite limit for the ransom, which is linked to the net worth of the individual or company covered by the contract, the broker of the K&R insurance policy advises the client on appropriate levels of coverage when it is purchased, so that the client does not pay a premium disproportionate to their net worth.

In principle, K&R insurance for journalists is no different from that taken out by other individuals or companies in other areas of work. However, it is often more difficult to obtain at a reasonable price because of the more fragmented nature of the media industry and how journalists work. Whereas an oil company may be able to tell brokers exactly who the policy will cover and in what locations, a media company may find it more difficult to do this beforehand.

Furthermore, over the past decade, the profile of journalists has changed. In the past, most combatants in international and civil conflicts were more likely to afford those identified as journalists – especially foreign journalists – some protection. Today, however, much coverage is being undertaken by local professional and citizen journalists who are perceived as opponents by some combatants. In some locations, foreign journalists from nations whose policies are at odds with combatants are increasingly perceived as surrogate targets for their governments. Because of these changes in profile and attitudes, media companies and journalists that may not previously have needed K&R insurance are (along with humanitarian/NGO workers) among the groups most at risk for kidnap and ransom demands.

Almost anyone can take out K&R insurance. However, it can be costly depending on the individuals and locations covered. Freelance journalists, for example, are often considered especially poor risks for underwriters because some have a reputation for taking greater risks in the field and not taking sensible precautions to minimise their risk profiles in both the physical and virtual worlds.

Underwriters may not agree to underwrite a policy if the profile of the person is too high because of the previous work they have done, the places they have been, the people they have worked with, and the risks they have faced. Much can be done to ensure that this does not happen, however, through the demonstration of risk awareness on the part of the insured and through proper planning and training.

Most reputable insurance brokers such as Marsh, Aon, Willis, JLT, and Lockton know where to obtain K&R insurance for their clients, whether with one of the Lloyds syndicates or the company markets such as AIG or Travelers. There are only about a dozen companies in the world who sit behind the insurers who provide the Lloyds market. The way these policies are worked out is via a line slip, a document provided by a broker to underwriters describing a prospective risk which allows them to determine what percentage of that risk they are prepared to underwrite. The lead underwriter takes the lion's share and then the broker fills the rest of the slip with other markets.

Confidentiality underpins K&R policies. Companies do not want to make their journalists more vulnerable by letting it be known that they have coverage or they may face demands for higher ransoms. Therefore, it is impossible to determine which media organisations have it. Even individuals within media firms who are covered by the policies typically do not know in case it compromises their safety or can lead to demands should they reveal it under interrogation if kidnapped. To help maintain this confidentiality, all policies are anonymous, being identified by codes, and all are dealt with offshore with what one consultant describes as a 'light IT touch'. This means that there should be no clear audit trail for K&R insurance and there should be no computer records linking the policy with the subject. There are two reasons for this: first, security-wise, those covered could become a target and second, from a legal perspective, paying ransoms is illegal in many jurisdictions. Brokers place the policies with underwriters who will not have contact with the insured companies or individuals.

As previously noted, the cost of policies varies extensively depending on location and persons covered. Coverage for an oil company executive in Colombia may cost less than for a journalist in Syria, who has the highest exposure and the least infrastructure support. Broadly speaking, coverage for a wealthy family in Latin America, where the risk of kidnap is relatively high, might cost £5,000 annually for a policy that provides £5 million of coverage. A policy provision for corporations might cost them £50,000 for a global policy with £10 to £50 million of cover.[1] There is no standard industry price for journalistic coverage available.

Globally, kidnap and ransom premiums amount to £500 million or £750 million annually, which indicates that it is in fact quite a niche market and perhaps suggests that many organisations do not in fact have these policies in place. As noted earlier, because of the secrecy surrounding

K&R policies, it is not possible to know how many media organisations have such policies, although some of the major news companies almost certainly do. Others may decide to forego polices and self-insure against the risk of kidnap, depending on what they estimate costs for handling kidnappings and the ransom payment might be. This may also be because the prevalence of long-term kidnappings is becoming less common – in part because of the impact of social media which means that information often gets out about the incident early – and also because of the changing tactics of kidnappers as evidenced by fundamentalist groups in the Middle East and North Africa over the past decade or so. In the past, kidnappings were negotiated over a long period of time, often years, but today many fundamentalist groups are employing new tactics.

Consultancy and crisis team activities

When kidnappings occur, a consultancy firm, which is always named on an insurance policy document, immediately begins working with the company and/or family of the insured victim. News organisations without K&R insurance can also access consultancy services by directly contracting with them if a kidnapping occurs (a selected list is included in Appendix 3).

Consultancies tend to operate in a similar manner and offer a 24/7 response through supporting call centres. There are a relatively small number of organisations which provide this expert level of support, and each of them tends to be contracted to one of the major underwriters. Consultancy firms are typically staffed by former police, intelligence, and military special operations personnel because of their investigative abilities and the high level of trust that is put in them by insurers. 'Because they are contracted by the insurers to manage the claim, so the insureds won't get their money back if we don't say so. Also, because we sit behind very many insurance policies, we manage loads of cases, not just K&R but also other critical security risks; so we know our stuff and can get things sorted swiftly', said one consultant, who asked to remain anonymous.

As soon as a kidnapping is suspected, a confirmation phase begins, during which the consultants confirm that the kidnapping has taken place, which triggers the policy. They then talk to the insured or contracting media company and the family. Underwriters allow immediate support, so a consultant can deploy rapidly to the location where the crisis management team will be centred. In some cases, two consultant

27

teams may be deployed – one to the place where the victim was working and the other to the headquarters where strategy is decided.

Consultants and the insured or contracting parties typically form a joint crisis management team. If clients have undergone preventative training, have contingency plans in place, or have dealt with previous kidnappings, this initial phase may proceed quicker. It is worth noting that underwriters often allow a percentage of the premium to be used for preventative training and preparation.

Responding to a kidnapping is enormously time-consuming for the consultants, the media organisation, and the families of victims. The crisis management team typically includes representatives of the media firm and the consultancy firm. It may or may not include a representative of the family because the work adds stress to the highly emotional situation. The decision is unique to each situation and depends upon the people in the family. If they are team members, they need to be full partners, but some negative intelligence and emotionally charged news may need to be disclosed carefully because of its potential to cause further psychological pain for relatives. If a family member is not included, there should be provisions in place to ensure an open line of communication with them so that they are kept informed and to ensure that they are supportive of strategies and efforts being used.

The media company needs to make a quick decision regarding who is going to represent it during kidnappings, whether an editor, publisher, or someone else. 'They need time, good judgment, and excellent organisational skills and dedication', says Philip Balboni of the GlobalPost, based on his experience of dealing with the Foley kidnapping.[2]

The size of the crisis management/kidnap resolution team may depend on the number of journalists being held hostage, the number of news organisations involved, the location of the kidnapping, and its duration. It may be very small when only one journalist is involved, but larger if two or more are involved. When more than one media enterprise is involved, more than one security firm may be involved as well.

A crucial step in forming the team is the appointment of one individual as the communicator, and the public dissemination of their name. This step is extremely important in this age of digital and social media because the hostage takers may want to contact and build a relationship with this individual. The consultants will then coach the named person. At this early stage, considerations are often less about the negotiations and more about issues such as information management.

This has to be managed at every level within the organisation and also with the family so that there is not too much 'chatter' that might compromise or increase the complexity of the situation. In this regard, those individuals and institutions linked to the incident have moral obligations to ensure that they do not put their hostage or other hostages at greater risk. An internal communication policy is just as important as an external one.

Among the first tasks of the consultant or consultants is to determine whether the journalist is alive and who is holding the journalist. The consultancy and crisis management team seeks out information and constantly evaluates sources of information and their credibility in doing so.

Obtaining that basic information is difficult in locations where chaotic conditions and multiple potential abductors might be involved. 'When someone was snatched you used to know who to negotiate with. Now you often have no idea who or where these people are or it takes vital time to find out', says Deborah Rayner, Senior Vice President of International News Gathering, TV and Digital at CNN International. 'In the world before you had nominally good guys and bad guys. You knew the leaders. If something went wrong you had direct contacts. Our fear now is it is harder to know who has them and where they are being held. There's often no obvious frontline anymore.'[3]

Over time, the focus moves to issues such as where the journalist is being held and how to communicate with those holding the journalist. Communication, whether direct or indirect through intermediaries, is important because it is used to establish a proof of life and to ascertain that the team is dealing with the people who actually hold the journalist and that ransom demands are not a scam by someone who is not involved.

The consultancy and crisis management team must constantly evaluate sources of information and their credibility. Information is obtained by interviewing people in the field and those who may have been held and released by the same kidnappers or had contact with the journalist in captivity.

False information and disappointments can arise, particularly in high-conflict regions involving multiple combatant groups. During the abduction of James Foley, for example, those seeking to free him believed for more than a year that he was taken by militia associated with the Assad regime. They were so certain of the veracity of the information that at one point they publicly accused the government of holding him or complicity in his holding.

Once the identity of kidnappers is determined and the location or general location where the journalist is being held is established, the crisis management team must deal with questions about what options exist to obtain release, how one would go about them, and who or what they would involve. It is important that the media organisation and families have a strong relationship with the consultancy personnel, but best practice requires that the media firm and family retain control of these decisions because they will live with their consequences.

Ransom issues

There is no easy answer to the question of whether ransoms should be paid. There is a potential that ransoms could be accepted by the kidnappers and the victim then not returned or killed, or that the ransom money gets into the hands of people not involved in the actual kidnapping. Payments are also complicated depending upon government policies regarding ransoms, as discussed in the previous chapter. Some governments accept company and insurance policy payments of ransoms to recover journalists from their countries and some will use government funds to help pay ransoms. Other countries discourage or forbid the payment of ransoms, arguing that it encourages more kidnappings, may involve negotiating with terrorists, and can fund terrorism and illegal activities.

In the UK and other countries that do not support the payment of a ransom, consultants often have to race to get to the family or company before the government does. 'If they get there first, they will establish the ground rules which never countenance financial resolution (ransom payment), thereby putting the victim at a distinct disadvantage; as pretty much all successful resolutions involve a cash settlement', according to one K&R consultant, who asked not to be named.

In terms of negotiations, the client decides whether to pay a ransom and the consultant advises. There can be some issues around paying too quickly as so-called 'double dips' have occurred, in which the hostage taker demands a second payment because the client paid the first so quickly they suspect they have easy access to more funds.

Demands made by kidnappers can be quite high. The captors of Peter Theo Curtis in Syria in 2012 demanded ransom payments as high as $25 million and Jim Foley's captors demanded $132.5 million from his parents and political concessions from the US government prior to killing him.

These levels of ransom amounts are typically reduced during negotiations, which can be quite lengthy because they are not held face to face and may involve intermediaries. The process is time-consuming and often frustrating, even when those holding hostages are doing so primarily for purposes of ransom.[4] When governments pay large ransoms, it raises kidnappers' expectations of the value of hostages, making it difficult for families or companies to raise sufficient funds for ransom.[5]

In 2015, the United Nations estimated that the Islamic State militant group (ISIS) received £28 million in ransom payments in the previous 12 months from various kidnappings of journalists and other civilians, leading security officials to argue that such payments were an important source of funding for weapons purchases and terrorist activities.

In late 2014, in the wake of a number of high-profile kidnapping incidents, the British Home Secretary Theresa May announced that she was seeking to close a loophole that allowed UK insurers to reimburse ransom payments made by companies.

In an article in the *Guardian* on 24 November 2014, Nicholas Watt and Alan Travis wrote:

> *There is no suggestion that UK-based insurers are helping to reimburse ransom money. But May thinks the Terrorism Act 2000, which criminalises all terrorist financing, has left a loophole as it does not explicitly ban UK insurance and reinsurance firms from reimbursing payments – even when they have reasonable cause to suspect that a payment could have been made to meet a terrorism demand.*[6]

The position of governments on ransoms is often questioned by consultants, who say it is more about playing a political game because the governments may also need to encourage individuals and companies to invest in areas which are high risk.

However, money is often not easy to come by for ransoms, even if the client has supporters. Cash is usually required and that much cash potentially contravenes money-laundering regulations. In addition to that challenge, transferring money in and out of countries is quite a skill. Nowadays, the way money is handed over can be a real test of nerves for the consultant, as it is often simply a case of dumping a bag of cash in a bin or deserted place and then the consultant must wait for the hostage taker or his/her contact to retrieve it, which may take days if they are being tracked.

The debate about whether media organisations should pay ransoms and whether they encourage subsequent kidnappings is a thorny one. The questions go far beyond the immediate organisational response to an individual kidnapping, and should be considered well before such an event, as part of the news organisation's contingency planning. Paying ransoms is undesirable for many reasons, but the alternatives – lengthened captivity, extended torment, and death – are dreadful.

Whether paying ransoms actually encourages more kidnapping is debatable. Some point to flurries of journalist captivity for ransom, particularly in places such as Afghanistan, Somalia, and Syria; others point out that many kidnappers seize journalists as hostages for political reasons and that ransoms can sometimes overcome those political motives. Organisational K&R insurance is a protective tool. Whether companies have it is unknown to those taking hostages, so it is unlikely that the insurance itself encourages individual kidnappings. K&R insurance, in fact, was only developed after kidnappings emerged as a real and significant threat.

Nevertheless, it is clear that habitual payment of ransoms perpetuates kidnappings in some regions. The idea of ending ransom payments is both controversial and morally charged because of its real immediate effects. If everyone suddenly refused to pay ransoms, hostage takers would likely respond and immediately increase the number of hostages killed.

Concerns over ransoms funding terrorist activities are not unfounded because the majority of hostage taking involves groups designated as terrorists by national governments and intergovernmental organisations. If ransoms were unavailable, however, they would undoubtedly find other ways to make their money – through bank robberies, gun running, drug dealing, prostitution, etc. In fact, most groups use a variety of these methods to raise funds and don't rely primarily on ransoms.

The decisions taken by news organisations of whether to pay ransoms are not simple and there is no best practice for making those choices. Whatever responsibility and pressure editors and publishers sense when their journalists are taken pales by comparison to the fright and anxiety felt by families and loved ones who will do everything possible to obtain the release of the journalist. All of these emotional pressures come into play during decisions of whether to pay ransoms, as well as the information and best advice available from security consultancies and organisational crisis teams.

Ransom payments

If a decision to pay a ransom is made, undertaking the transaction presents a host of difficulties involving what currencies, precious metals, gems, or other valuable commodities will be used, where it will be delivered, and whether the kidnappers will receive it directly or through an intermediary. Many things can go wrong during the ransom payment process, including kidnappers calling off the delivery out of concern for their safety and ransoms being lost or taken by other individuals. In addition, there is always the risk that the kidnappers will take the money and not free the victim.

Most ransom payments and deliveries are made remotely, without direct contact with the kidnappers. 'You dump cash in a bag in a bin, or chuck it out of an aircraft in a waterproof sack and hope for the best', said one expert, who requested anonymity.

Releases of hostages

The release of kidnap victims takes place in many ways. Some are released at locations where they can walk away from kidnappers and seek help. Some are released to intermediaries. Often the method and location are not subject to negotiation. Methods of release tend to be similar even in cases where negotiations and ransom payments are not involved.

'Victims are often hurled out of a moving car in front of a hotel (in marine cases, usually abandoned on board their ships)', says one security consultant who requested anonymity, adding: 'the old telly image of steely-eyed negotiators eyeballing the bad guys across a bridge with the victim walking towards a bag of money are long gone'.

When a kidnap victim is released, it is important for the news organisation or their representatives to swiftly remove them from the location, lest kidnappers change their mind or they fall prey to others who would like to benefit. When consultants are involved they often undertake the rapid movement of the released journalist, but at times this is done by the news organisation itself.

The relief of the release does not end the organisational response, however. The organisation subsequently must attend to medical, psychological, and other needs of the journalist and their families/loved ones. Depending upon the nature of the individual kidnapping, the organisation may need to spend both time and resources to aid in the individual's recovery and return to work.

4

Experiencing Kidnapping

Every kidnapping is different. What journalists, their employers, and their families experience depends upon where the individuals are kidnapped, the perpetrators, the length of captivity, their nationality, and many other factors. Nevertheless, things can be learned from their experiences. In this chapter, four journalists who experienced and survived kidnappings, and their families/loved ones, tell their stories. The first two focus on the actual events surrounding their kidnappings and what it is like to be held. The second two focus on the effects on families and the aftermath of the kidnapping.

Getting individuals who have been kidnapped to discuss their captivity is a complicated business for a number of reasons. These include the fact that often the episodes were so traumatic that they would prefer not to revisit them. Some suffer from forms of post-traumatic stress that affect their physical and mental states and behaviour long after the precipitating events. Others feel that they have already revisited them to the point of exhaustion and they have nothing more to add, even if they are speaking with different people.

The cases presented here, and conversations both on and off the record with other former kidnapped journalists, make it clear that the families and loved ones of those journalists need support from other family, friends, and the journalists' employers and colleagues, and the journalistic community as a whole, during and after kidnappings (some resources for families are found in Appendix 2).

Speaking with the relatives or loved ones of those kidnapped is in many ways even more complicated because often they are less prepared to face the limelight than their media relatives and because they also want to move on with their lives once the incident is over. Additionally, they tend not to get as much support in the aftermath of the kidnapping as those who have been through it. They also suffer psychological trauma during kidnappings that can lead to post-traumatic stress disorder and it is important that they seek support in dealing with its effects.

All of these challenges arise when trying to collate information and interviews from those who have been kidnapped and those whose loved ones have been kidnapped. What is less evident is also the fact that where journalists have carried on visiting hostile environments, talking publicly about their experiences may raise their own risk profile in future journalistic endeavours and that of their employing companies, which in turn may be costly, and not just from a financial perspective.

For the purposes of this chapter, we have explored the experiences of journalists who have been kidnapped using a number of sources, including several extended interviews with individuals who agreed to be named and to talk in detail about their experiences. The cases presented here provide insight into how kidnappings take place, what happens during captivity, the effects that these episodes have on families and loved ones of victims, and what is needed for these different sets of individuals during and after kidnapping. These discussions yield some important lessons for journalists and their families caught up in kidnappings, some of which are summarised in the box below.

Lessons from journalists' kidnappings

Lessons for journalists

The following basic suggestions may help journalists avoid kidnapping before it happens. (More exhaustive suggestions and tactics are usually provided in safety training programmes.)

- Take hostile environment/safety training.
- Be aware of the dangers in your location.
- Plan your activities carefully.
- Complete a risk assessment; have and understand the contingency plans in place (both of your own and your media organisation).
- Consider details that might help in the event that proof of life needs to be determined.
- Make sure your employer and family know where you are and who you are meeting.
- Have a communications plan in place, with contact numbers and Next of Kin (NOK) details left with your employer and colleagues in the field.

- Be wary of who you work with – do as much due diligence as possible, but also be aware that individuals and groups may change their allegiances without warning.
- Ensure that your social media profile does not compromise your safety.
- Carry clean laptops, phones, etc.; think about using aliases for contacts.
- Do not make yourself a target. Blend in so that you are not easily identifiable as a journalist when travelling.
- Understand what your employer and colleagues will be doing on your behalf.
- Do what you have to do to survive and escape.
- Understand that kidnappings are traumatic and require recovery time and counselling afterwards.

Lessons for families

- Seek help from the employer, safety organisations, expert and support groups, governments, and neutral parties.
- Expect information to be incomplete and irregular.
- Be prepared for emotional highs and lows during the process.
- Understand that effects of kidnapping do not end upon release. You and your loved one may benefit from trauma counselling afterwards.

The experience of Anthony Loyd, *The Times*

Anthony Loyd, a journalist for *The Times* newspaper, was kidnapped in Syria in 2014, beaten by his captors, and then shot as he tried to escape. The reporter was betrayed by a man called Hakim, whom he had used as a source over the course of two years of travelling in and out of the country.

Loyd, his photographer colleague Jack Hill, and their Syrian fixer Mahmoud were staying at Hakim's house in the town of Tar Rifaat on what was supposed to be their last night in Syria.

Figure 1 Anthony Loyd

I think the relationship of the guy who betrayed me was mischaracterised as a friendship. The relationship was based on trust and he was a good source of information. I happened to quite like him and I think he quite liked me and Jack.

Loyd says he had no sense of the imminent betrayal that was about to deprive them of their freedom.

He was typical of a low-middle ranking commander: he knew a little bit about how war worked, but every man can turn bad over time. I always thought, given the dynamics of the war, that it was possible Hakim or someone like him might one day try to sell us out, but I thought I might get some hint of the change in dynamics before it happened.

The journalist has given much thought as to whether he could have avoided the kidnapping. He says he could say that he should not have stayed that final night to congratulate Hakim on the birth of his newest child, a daughter, but he also stayed to cultivate the relationship, as Hakim had in the past been a good source and a reliable host. He had dismissed the local security he and his team had been using for the past five days because Hakim had his own security.

I knew he had a dodgy side, but I tend to think it was a difficult situation to avoid. I had sent away our local security because Hakim's guys were bigger, badder, and better armed.

Loyd is no stranger to risk and adversity. He is a veteran of many conflicts over the past 20 years and he says that some of his previous experience of war reporting inevitably fed into the way he reacted when he was kidnapped. In addition, he knew some of the threats he was facing, citing a near abduction in Syria in 2012 when his security outfit of eight men was confronted by three ISIS fighters. 'We got out of that situation eventually, only as we knew the doctor who was treating the ISIS guys', he noted.

On the more recent occasion, Loyd and his team were leaving Tar Rifaat and heading back to the Syrian border with Turkey when their passage was blocked by a shiny dark SUV which seemed out of place on the dusty roads. Minutes later, when his team was dragged out of the car and spread-eagled, it became quite clear to him that the men who were kidnapping him had done this before.

When we saw the car that was going to take us, it was very bad news. I had set the tracker and had the safety arm ready to go. When the bad shit happened a few seconds later I thought, 'this bit is ugly, don't freeze, this is the bad shit, stay with it and don't leave it.'

He says he is not sure if this reaction came from lessons learnt on Hostile Environment (HE) courses or from his previous experiences.

This episode occurred in early 2014. Many journalists were being held at that time in Syria, some of whom were known about publicly and some whose abduction was subjected to media blackouts. Loyd was aware of the dangers facing journalists, even if at this stage they had not quite reached the levels they would in late 2014, when James Foley and Steven Sotloff were murdered by ISIS militants who filmed their beheadings. Loyd says he was aware of the gravity of the situation as soon as he was taken and the absolute necessity of escape.

Obviously I knew that journalists were being taken and thought that the killings would start after the air strikes began. I knew that we had to escape and that was a very conscious thing. If you don't, you get stuck in an environment where it feels too dangerous to escape, but if you don't try to then you might get murdered. You are aware of the sense that you might feel safer doing nothing but need to rescind that train of thought.

There were elements of shock which I think I endured and I am not sure if that was HE or experience on the road. There was a logic to it, but as to any organised plan as to how I was going to get out of it, I was grasping at it.

After being passed from one group to another, Loyd was flung into the back of a car, where he was blindfolded and beaten. Still he kept thinking about his escape.

He said one of the hardest things in terms of trying to figure out how he might escape was the fact he was separated from his team and was unable to communicate with them. Jack and Mahmoud had been put in the boot of the car and both had been handcuffed. Because Mahmoud had been detained before, he had had the foresight to angle his forearms out slightly, which in turn allowed him to release his hands. The team that was guarding the two men had opened the boot of the car where they were being held to allow them to breathe. As they did so Mahmoud recognised one of Hakim's security guards. He helped Jack release his arms, leapt on the guard, and started clubbing him with a hammer.

At this stage Loyd was in the back seat of the car, completely unaware of what was going on just inches from him. 'All I can hear is this guy is being hit with a blunt object and I thought it was one of us being beaten.' He said the next few minutes were very confusing. He heard whispering, made out Jack's voice urging him to run, and pushed open the door of the car from which he was finally able to escape. Disorientated and unable to see his colleagues anywhere, he noticed a shard of sunlight through the ceiling and made a run for it.

Having had time to think about the escape since, Loyd reflects that this was not a group plan but one member of the team seizing a chance, involving another member of the group he couldn't communicate with, and then a third who they couldn't see.

I felt like thinking, 'thanks a lot guys you left me behind,' but I understand why they did it. In hindsight, I understand why as soon as they overcame the guard Mahmoud made a run for it. I assumed that the dreadful struggle that I heard was our guys.

Loyd suggests that future hostile environment training courses should consider advising journalists that, if they are kidnapped and do get the chance to escape, it is unlikely that they will be able to plan it in advance so they should consider code words and what they might do in advance.

Even after his escape, Loyd was not safe. He was detained again, enduring horrific beatings, was shot twice by Hakim and then underwent shameful treatment at the hands of those who held him. He finally ended up in a field clinic, where he was told he was safe. From there he was moved to a hospital where he was treated and within hours he was free and taken back across the border with his colleagues to Turkey.

The team had been taken at 8.30 in the morning, when they were 20 minutes from the border and their agreed rendezvous with a security adviser. When they failed to make this meeting, the security adviser called the newspaper, which in turn called Loyd's wife.

> It happened very quickly. The logic was that we were not sure how it would end and they wanted to keep her abreast of the situation. She received several calls from The Times while I was being cleaned and patched up.

Loyd says that there was a plan in place to deal with the eventuality of kidnap and, even though the incident did not last more than a day, he believes this was extremely important.

> We had a good plan, a security guy on the border and a translator who had a checklist of people to call, including the headquarters of the Islamic Front. The Islamic Front gave them a couple of gunmen and they drove to Tal Rifaat, where we had left that morning. There was a febrile atmosphere. Our security adviser finds Mahmoud in a house with the hammer still and he is completely wigged out. Mahmoud cannot really articulate what has happened. He goes back and says there has been some kind of break-out and that call was reinterpreted to my wife.

Loyd's wife in turn had received a call from him after he had been given a phone in the hospital and told he could call someone.

> I sounded quite strange, sounded quite cold, didn't want to say I had been abducted … She then called The Times and told them something was wrong because [he, Loyd] sounded quite off his head. I had thought to myself whatever you do, you can't sound emotional, but in my effort not to sound choky, I sounded like I was speaking under duress. From my point of view at that stage things were good; I had had the chance to survive.

In addition to the plan in place on the border, *The Times* had a crisis management team in London, a process established after the death of *Sunday Times* reporter Marie Colvin in the Syrian city of Homs, that immediately brought together a group of decision-makers in the event of a crisis such as Loyd's kidnapping.

> *This was a group of civilians with loads of other responsibilities and they got through everything and did so in the first few hours, so rejecting the advice from [the experts] to let the dust settle. Me and my team also contributed dramatically to staying alive.*

However, even though the kidnapping itself was well dealt with by *The Times*, to which he is extremely grateful, Loyd says he struggled after he returned home.

> *The one bit that I didn't aim for was when I was discharged from hospital, when my wife goes back to work and kids go back to school, I felt a terrible shame. [You might say] why do you feel shame, you've survived? But I ended up naked, covered in blood which was oozing out of my eyeballs, my nose, my ears, they jumped on my gunshot injuries. I spent a long time at home, unable to walk, just staring at the ceiling, stuck with it.*

He said he would not put his reaction down to the effects of post-traumatic stress.

> *It was really humiliating, being treated like an animal. I would have liked a bit more support – use that word cautiously – I didn't want a barrage of shrinks. I wanted a wise person who was used to that kind of experience. I don't feel like I have a vestigial problem. I think I had some kind of vile experience and that will leave some sort of legacy.*

Loyd, whose wife is a trauma counsellor, did see an expert twice but did not feel the counsellor fully understood the experience.

> *He said, 'do you have a problem with gun fire, loud noises or flashbacks?' I thought 'no'. It was more the issue of humiliation, of being treated like an animal and the guilt of being the one who decided that the team should stay in that house that night. I wanted someone who was a bit more aware of the complexities of the situation.*

In terms of what could have been handled differently after the event, Loyd says he wished there had been an option to look at a different kind of therapy, as it took him four or five months to come to terms with what he had been through. He says he would also have liked the option for his wife to have had some kind of support.

Speaking almost a year on from his experience, he said he was eventually fit and did return to work, but when he did so he was treated with 'kid gloves … It would have been worse had they been callous, but I think *The Times* should have had a bit of sensible advice vis-à-vis how to deal with it. If I had not been agitating to go back to Iraq, I might not have gone.'

In the time since his release, he has also been able to reflect on the fortunate aspects of his experience, something thrown into sharp relief by the horrendous killings of journalists James Foley, Steven Sotloff, and Kenji Goto. The beheading of Foley in particular hit Loyd and his family hard, as he had been a friend.

Articulating how different his fate might have been, Loyd notes:

We would have been sold. When we used to think about all those who had been taken, realising how few of them had been originally taken by ISIS. Most were taken by renegade FSA [Free Syrian Army] groups and sold on. We were part of that horrible fulcrum point before journalists were beheaded and seen as fair game.

The challenges created by trading in hostages increases the risks to abducted journalists, even if they are originally detained or abducted by groups that have fewer capabilities for holding hostages for lengthy periods and are less willing to kill hostages in the pursuit of their objectives.

Tips for surviving a kidnapping

Over the years, security consultants have developed advice for people at risk for kidnappings. These include:

- Attempt to stop it by escaping when it initially occurs.
- Observe and note where you are and how you got there.
- Pay attention to kidnappers' demeanour, behaviour, and routines.
- Find out why the kidnappers want you.

- Cooperate once in captivity and do not insult your captors.
- Humanise yourself and keep your dignity.
- Try to establish rapport with some of the kidnappers.
- Communicate with any other captives.
- Stay mentally and physically active.
- Watch for signs that the situation is changing.
- Figure out how to protect yourself if a rescue attempt is made.
- Escape if you can and have opportunity to get to safety.

The experience of Miguel Medina, Agence France-Presse

Like Loyd, Miguel Medina, who works for Agence France-Presse, was kidnapped in Syria. The Colombian photojournalist was held in 2013 on the eleventh day of a three-week trip when he was covering Syria out of the Turkish border town of Kilis.

That day he received permission from his Paris headquarters to travel to Aleppo to cover the destruction of a minaret in the Syrian city.

Figure 2 Miguel Medina

Instead of travelling with his AFP colleagues, he went alone with his driver and fixer. He had been allowed to do so because he had already been to Syria several times and had established good connections with the rebels.

They began by visiting a refugee camp across the border in Syria, where they spent a couple of hours. They then drove to Azaz, close to Aleppo, where Medina wanted to stop for water to take with them.

> *There I saw a Syrian guy next to a Chevrolet from the 1950s and I wanted to take his photo, but at that moment four guys dressed in black stopped me. I usually look all around me to check my surroundings, but my first mistake was to get out of the car without looking around.*

He said the men stopped him, asked him for his papers and then took him into a small room,

> *where there were six men with AK-47s and the situation changed. One of them became very aggressive and said I was a spy and working for the Americans. I told him about my life and realised I now had to convince him I was not a spy.*
>
> *I started talking about history and literature, about my favourite authors: Dostoevsky, Faulkner and García Márquez. He asked me if I had read the Bible and I lied and said I had. He asked me if I had read the Qur'an and I said I had not. Then he said 'you read the students but you do not read the masters' and then I realised I could not relate to him in that way.*

Despite this, the man offered him tea and Medina asked him his age: 'I said I think you are a similar age to me, in your forties and if you kill me you will also kill my father, you will kill two people. He said he also had one other person in his life, his daughter. Then he said, I will let you go.'

Medina felt fortunate to have been able to establish such a relationship with this man, whom he believes may have been a doctor because 'he kept touching my heart to see if I was nervous, even though I tried to sound as calm as possible'.

He was released after being held for three hours and immediately called his colleagues in Paris before flying back there via Istanbul. He had not previously been able to alert them to his predicament because in the speed of the kidnapping he had not been able to hit the emergency button on his iPhone. The button is part of an app that starts sending the phone's GPS location and a message that the person carrying it is involved in an emergency situation.

Medina was confused about who had captured him, a problem that is common in conflicts involving multiple factions and one that often perplexes those seeking to recover journalists.

> At the beginning I thought it was Al-Nusra who had taken me, but now I believe it was Da'esh [Islamic State] because of the way they were with their weapons, their dress, their training. They were not the kind of rebels I met at the beginning in Syria. I think I was lucky because I am Colombian and I think it was because I was honest.

He says he is not sure who was responsible for selling him out. 'The fixer had an important father who was part of the Muslim Brotherhood. The driver was from Aleppo. In wars, a fixer is really someone who is there for the money, so I'm not sure if it was the fixer who sold me.'

Medina acknowledges that he made some mistakes. 'My first was not to look around when I got out the car and my second was to cross my legs and to show them the bottom of my shoes.' (Showing the sole of your shoe has long been considered an insult in Arab culture.)

On his return to Paris, the AFP offered him psychological help and although he said he felt he did not need it, he attended an appointment. For a couple of months after the incident, he decided not to return to conflict areas, but he has since covered a number of other types of stories. Speaking two years on from his kidnapping and in the wake of a number of killings of other journalists, he says he believes things could have ended very differently.

> Every person reacts in different ways. I am 47 years old. If I had that kind of trip between 25 and 30, it might have been very different. But now if I see something where I do not feel good about the risks then I won't do it. I see too many people who die and I wonder why they bring such sadness on their family. This is a problem with some of the media; they want to live this experience of war. I love my job. It is not that I am always prepared, because every war is different, but I know where my feet stand so I am not going to take any stupid risks. It is not necessary to risk my life for my photos.

The experience of Colin Freeman, the *Telegraph*

Figure 3   Colin Freeman

Like the previous two men described, Colin Freeman was a veteran journalist with more than a decade of experience when he was kidnapped in Somalia. The foreign correspondent for the *Telegraph* was kidnapped in Somalia and held for 40 days in 2008.

He and his photographer colleague Jose Cendon were taken hostage on the way to the airport for their flight home by the gunmen they had paid to protect them. Freeman had covered some of the world's most dangerous places over the decade prior to his kidnapping. He said his family had always worried a bit about the nature of his work and the threats to him since he started doing work in places like Iraq. On the other hand, because he had experience of working as the *Telegraph*'s foreign editor, he had a good sense of what the newspaper would do to manage such a crisis if it arose. He had been involved when a colleague was arrested in Zimbabwe and when another was kidnapped in Basra and forced to appear on camera.

Knowing the probable organisational response to his abduction helped him appreciate that he was not forsaken in his captivity and that his paper was working for his release. 'I knew there would be a crisis group in place and I knew what they would do in terms of other things like a media blackout.' However, he says he cannot ever remember sitting down with his family and explaining what would happen from the *Telegraph*'s perspective if he was ever kidnapped on newspaper business. 'What emerged when I was finally released was that my family was summoned in to see the paper within 24 to 36 hours and also introduced to the negotiating team trying to secure my release.'

He said he believes the *Telegraph* wanted to show his loved ones they 'were doing everything they could to try and get me released'. Freeman says the paper's representatives gave them some information, but 'the family were a little bit like rabbits in headlights – as my mum or sister put it, it felt a bit like a James Bond movie'.

In retrospect, he advises those who are running a news desk or sending colleagues to dangerous places that it is a good idea to tell their next of kin that the organisation will do their best to get them out in the event of a kidnapping, but that they will not be able to provide a running commentary and that involving the family in every decision may in fact complicate matters. He says it is also a good idea for journalists to agree with their news desks about who is to be kept in the loop if they are kidnapped and to do so before they are deployed.

> *My family did not know my girlfriend very well at the time and she was fretting about that. It is probably a sensible idea to give a crib sheet about who should be consulted and who should be avoided and who they would like to be kept informed. Usually you have a point of contact, which we had at the paper.*

He said that his family and girlfriend would get anxious if the paper's representatives told one of them one thing and another of them something slightly different in the course of conversation. 'They were understandably normal people and this is what stress brings out in you.'

> *It is best to do this before it happens rather than try to do this in the heat of the moment because it is remarkable how it is possible to misinterpret information because of the sheer lack of it. For instance if the paper had not rung by a certain time, my girlfriend would worry. Interpreting things is a symptom of the desperation people get in that situation.*

Freeman says that during their first visit to the paper, his relatives were told that the paper's representatives would not necessarily be able to provide them with information every day and they would have to take the *Telegraph* on trust to an extent. 'As time dragged on they were, generally speaking, quite patient as the paper did a good job of making them feel involved, but they wanted it to give more.' Freeman is not convinced that a more informative policy would have helped his family, saying: 'you worry no matter what information you are given'.

He says he thinks there are times when professional negotiating teams are probably much more open but he does not necessarily know if this might have been the case in his situation.

A checklist for families

- Immediately contact employer or contracting news organisation if you learn of the kidnapping from other sources.
- Select a family member to be the primary contact for the family and to work with the crisis team.
- Contact relevant government agencies for information and assistance.
- Select a spokesperson to handle media inquiries and to shield the family from those pressures.
- Be aware of the psychological stress the event causes and seek personal support from friends, clerics, and counsellors.

The experience of David Rohde, *New York Times*

The American journalist David Rohde was kidnapped by the Taliban in Afghanistan in 2008 with two local colleagues, reporter Tahir Ludin, and their driver, Asadullah Mangal. At the time, Rohde was researching a book and working for the *New York Times*.

In an article for the newspaper written shortly after his escape, Rohde said:

> *During our time as hostages, I tried to reason with our captors. I told them we were journalists who had come to hear the Taliban's side of the story. I told them that I had recently married and that Tahir and Asad had nine young children between them. I wept, hoping it would create sympathy, and begged them to release us. All of my efforts proved pointless.*[1]

Rohde eventually managed to escape after seven months in captivity. Looking back at the period during which he was held first in Afghanistan and then in the tribal areas of Pakistan, he wrote that: 'Over those months, I came to a simple realization. After seven years of reporting in the region, I did not fully understand how extreme many of the Taliban had become.'

During his detention, the *New York Times* liaised with other media outlets to ensure that news of his kidnapping was kept under a blackout. This happened even as his kidnappers demanded a hefty ransom, which the US government refused to pay. The issue of blackouts became hotly debated afterwards.

Rohde himself says:

I believe it was the security consultant who suggested it and the Times embraced the approach; I do not think it made a difference. The kidnappers were so delusional. They were just convinced I was worth a huge amount of money. I don't think blackouts work. I don't think going public works. I think that having several million dollars works. One of the unintended consequences was that people did not know the full extent of the threats to journalists.

Rohde, who had been married for just two months when he was kidnapped, says that while his new wife Kristen Mulvihill had the support of his news organisation, the service provided by the various security consultants differed in quality. Some of what they said turned out to be false because they were relying too heavily on informants who were not telling the truth. This proved difficult because it raised her hopes and those of his family before crushing them.

Rohde had left a phone number and the name of the Taliban commander whom he was interviewing with the bureau chief of *The Times*, giving his paper a good place to start looking for him. However, both he and his wife say that one of the key sources of information came from the established network of journalists that he had from decades of working in the profession and this was in fact superior to the information provided by the government and the FBI.

Since his escape, Rohde has worked with the families of other journalists who have been kidnapped. Looking to the current situation in Syria, he says that the 'huge frustration' there is not being able to rely on an information network from colleagues, as there is so little information because so few journalists are able to work there safely.

Mulvihill, who co-authored a book with Rohde on their experience, says that for her it was a very steep learning curve, even though she had been to the region with Rohde. Like her husband, she credits the support and help of his colleagues. She also says that she valued the support and experience of former Taliban hostage Jere Van Dyk. 'He told me they would not hurt him physically, and that he would be treated as a guest, as the Pashtunwali were holding him. I was a little annoyed about that but having seen what happened in Syria since, then I am thankful.'

She also spoke with the former hostage and BBC reporter Alan Johnston. 'He said the outcome was not going to be up to us, not from a false move that David made. It was helpful to touch base with people who had survived because it was a very isolating experience.'

Mulvihill, who also works in the media, had just started a new job when her husband was kidnapped. She paid tribute to her editor-in-chief at *Cosmopolitan* magazine where she was a picture editor, saying that she told her about the kidnapping and that she abided by the blackout and did not tell anyone, as well as giving her the support she needed when she had to take time off, or make calls or attend meetings with those involved in the negotiations.

She said she initially felt a little guilty working, especially as it was regularly interrupted, but it gave her some measure of control and routine. In addition, she was able to draw on the help of her family members, and she was grateful that her mother kept things going at home and made sure she was eating and sleeping, so she could work and then spend time at night dealing with the kidnapping.

Rohde had been detained previously in Bosnia in the 1990s and therefore his brother was extremely helpful as he had prior experience of dealing with his detention. 'He had been through that and he managed the information flow to the family. He absorbed a lot of that', Mulvihill says, noting that it helped a great deal because at times the wider family were very frustrated and also angry with Rohde.

In terms of how she maintained her resilience for the seven-month period, Mulvihill says it was initially hard to have peace of mind. She had always prayed, though not in the traditional way, and now she fell back on a more traditional approach to prayer.

They provided me with words when I did not have my own. I said a prayer for him. It was one of the hymns from our wedding. I said it to stay connected with him. I tried to avoid imagining his surroundings, though

afterwards he said he could picture exactly where I was and recall trips
we had taken together.

As well as the support from her family, she did have support from the
FBI and an offer of seeing a counsellor, but she did not feel comfortable
doing so. Instead she found a therapist in New York who specialised
in post-traumatic stress disorder treatment and she found that helpful.
She was also introduced to a book after several months that she found
very helpful. The publication, by James Alvarez, is called *The Psychological
Impact of Kidnap*. She has since recommended it to the families of others
who have been kidnapped.

However, it was not always easy. During Rohde's detention, the
Mumbai terror attacks occurred and Mulvihill says she found it difficult,
'because she did not know if the silence from the kidnappers meant that
they were involved'.

The FBI was involved from the first day. Mulvihill says: 'I do think
the FBI had the best channel to the kidnappers in terms of producing
proof of life videos, despite the fact that this was not obvious early on.' She
said that she found their role frustrating at times during the kidnapping
and only really appreciated them in retrospect. She also acknowledges that
the FBI kept them informed after Rohde's kidnapping had ended, to the
extent that they told the family that one of the perpetrators had been
killed in an air strike before it was made public.

They were very good about training me from the start of the negotiations.
They told me what to do if I got a call – they were reassuring me because
the unknown is the worst.

She also said that she had tremendous support from Richard
Holbrooke, then the US Special Representative for Afghanistan and
Pakistan: 'He raised the issue of the kidnap every time he went over there
and it helped bring visibility with the authorities when David escaped and
we had to get him out of Pakistan.'

Speaking of the media blackout, Mulvihill says that she and her
brother-in-law were in the main responsible for the decision about not
going public, and that they agreed that if they ever thought the government
was not doing enough, then they would have done so.

'We worried about him being the next Daniel Pearl and we did not
want him to be the next PR pawn' is the main reason she gives for holding

firm on the blackout. Seeing the way cases have played out since then in Syria, she believes there would have been more room for error had they gone public.

Looking back to the period of time before Rohde was taken, she says he had undertaken an 'embed' (involving a journalist attaching to a combat unit of a party in a conflict) immediately prior to his kidnapping and they were more worried about that. However, when he called her several times the day he went to do the interview, she says she thought something was up. Although she did not know exactly what he was planning, she was surprised that he used a fixer he had not worked with before. However, the fixer actually turned out to be very helpful.

'I knew that ambition was coming into it', she says of the decision by the man she had recently married to go to Afghanistan, though he had promised it would be his last trip there. 'I was a little annoyed at the start, but he endured a lot for what he decided to do.'

These four experiences reveal the different aspects of how kidnappings take place and affect those involved. They provide compelling confirmation of the need for journalists and organisations to be prepared for the potential ordeal and how they will respond during and following a kidnapping.

5

Coverage of Journalist Kidnappings

The ways in which the kidnapping of journalists is covered by the news media raises significant questions about what information is conveyed, the sources of the information, whether journalists' kidnappings should be handled differently from other abductions, whether journalists and news organisations pay more attention to the kidnappings of their own, and whether they are more willing to engage in news blackouts when journalists are involved.

This chapter looks at general law enforcement–media relations, how the media typically report kidnappings in civil and conflict settings, provides examples of how kidnappings are covered by the media, shows differences in coverage for journalists and other types of individuals who are detained, and discusses the implications of the coverage. It shows that there are significant ethical issues involved in choices that media organisations make and provides ways to think about those decisions.

The traditional relationship between the media and law enforcement agencies is delicate even in domestic settings in stable democratic countries. The media not only report on public events to which law enforcement and security agencies respond, but they also have a duty to question and hold accountable such bodies for their performance and use or abuse of power.[1] In the course of normal police–media interactions, police control accident, disaster, and crime scenes to which media want access and they control information released about events to protect the privacy of individuals involved and aid prosecution efforts. In addition, police departments use information to control their images and legitimacy by trying to influence how they and crime news are presented.[2]

These general tensions between police and media are compounded when kidnappings, hostage takings, or terrorist acts are involved. Journalists covering such events are attempting to get as much information as possible from any sources available and to document the event with live and recorded video and photographs.[3] These basic journalistic functions, however, may interfere with the immediate resolution of the event or the follow-up investigation. Authorities are particularly concerned about coverage that may endanger civilians or police or otherwise complicate their responses to the events. These conflicting purposes and concerns of police/security forces and the media are also found in coverage involving the seizure or abduction of journalists.

During ongoing events such as sieges, hostage takings, and kidnappings, police are particularly concerned about live broadcasts of information that might reveal strategies or tactics of police to perpetrators, show movements and preparations of police forces, and any coverage that might complicate or compromise their abilities to control the scene or might interfere with negotiations that may be under way.[4] The media were heavily criticised, for example, when some of the coverage of the 2015 lethal attack on journalists at the French satirical magazine *Charlie Hebdo* and the subsequent supermarket siege in Paris broadcast live the movements and positioning of police. Some members of the media made telephone calls to interview the supermarket perpetrator. These actions were condemned for endangering police, interfering with efforts to resolve the situation, and violating national broadcast policies. They also resulted in lawsuits against media organisations by survivors.[5]

Despite concerns about media coverage involving hostage takings and terrorist acts in stable domestic settings,[6] little agreement exists among authorities and media organisations on guidelines for covering such events.[7] Some news organisations have independently created internal policies for handling them.[8] Most security agencies and news organisations, however, do not have separate policies or guidelines for handling kidnappings of journalists, and most media tend to fall back on their general policies when covering kidnappings of journalists employed by other news organisations in these settings.

Although some journalist kidnappings take place in locations where local authorities are able to exercise police power, the majority of journalist kidnappings today take place where local authority is diminished or absent and the democratic values of the press do not prevail. Nevertheless, the same basic concerns about media coverage remain: will it endanger the victims or others? Will it complicate efforts to obtain their release?

Coverage in different settings

In considering how the kidnapping of journalists is covered by the news industry, one must first examine the issues surrounding media coverage of kidnappings generally and the issues of kidnappings related to combatants engaged in conflicts. When kidnappings take place in relatively stable social settings, they generally involve individuals seized for ransom or seized during the staging of crimes to which police authorities respond to resolve and investigate. These episodes can occasionally involve journalists, as was the case in 2006 when a reporter and technician from TV Globo were kidnapped by a Brazilian criminal gang to gain coverage of poor prison conditions.[9]

Kidnappings of civilians and journalists also take place in unstable locations where authority is absent and open combat exists. These sometimes involve criminal motives, but most often involve capture and detention by armed forces for military or political reasons. Kidnappings also take place in areas not war-torn, but where local authority has been destabilised and weakened by drug and other criminal cartels and political corruption, problems that have led to a significant number of journalist kidnappings in Latin American countries.

Kidnappings in stable social settings

When civilians are kidnapped in stable social settings, journalists and news organisations must balance a variety of competing interests. They must respond to the public's interest in being informed about community developments while at the same time attending to the public interest in the protection and safe recovery of victims. They typically wish to support the public interest in capturing and prosecuting perpetrators, while at the same time observing and assessing the activities and effectiveness of law enforcement and criminal justice personnel. Journalists need to obtain information from family members and friends, but need to avoid unduly increasing the pressure and fear the family and friends are experiencing because of the events.

Kidnappings in civil settings are often carried out for ransom, although many involve domestic custody disputes. A smaller number involve sexual deviants or individuals seeking children. Media tend to cover each of these types of crimes slightly differently, depending upon the information available to them from authorities and family members.

Studies of the media's coverage of kidnappings have shown that some kidnappings get different and varying amounts of coverage than others for a number of reasons.[10] At times, the coverage is constrained because of a lack of information and the absence of confirmation from law enforcement or families; at other times, it is unreserved because of the involvement of public figures or sympathetic victims or family members willing to talk with media. Issues of class, gender, and race also affect the amount and nature of coverage. Cases of kidnappings involving young children, persons of privilege, and Caucasians are more likely to get significant news coverage than kidnappings involving older individuals or people from lower classes and from other ethnic groups. This problem is found in most crime coverage. Separate studies of coverage of kidnappings of journalists are limited, but large Western media have been criticised for putting greater emphasis on kidnappings of journalists from their own countries or other Western countries and for a tendency to provide minimal coverage or ignore kidnappings of journalists from other parts of the world.

There is no standard practice for covering kidnappings of civilians. Most news organisations and smaller police agencies often do not have well-established policies specifically for dealing with them even in stable developed nations. Locations such as large metropolitan areas may, over time, experience kidnappings more often and this may induce their police agencies and media to establish working guidelines on coverage, but these tend to be relatively broad because the nature of kidnappings and demands of kidnappers vary significantly. None of these specifically address kidnappings of journalists.

Although not specifically addressing kidnappings, the section on minimising harm in the Society of Professional Journalists' Code of Ethics is particularly germane in cases of kidnapping:

> Ethical journalism treats sources, subjects, colleagues and members of the public as human beings deserving of respect. Journalists should ... [b]alance the public's need for information against potential harm or discomfort. Pursuit of the news is not a license for arrogance or undue intrusiveness.[11]

In general, good practice encourages journalists to provide only basic information during a kidnapping, withholding any information that may lead to additional harm to the victim or assist the perpetrators in escaping, and to avoid media frenzy and hysteria in coverage. At times, media outlets may even refrain from reporting the kidnapping until after its conclusion at the request of authorities, particularly in cases where children or entire families are being held.[12]

A particularly challenging issue occurs because media outlets may, at times, be asked to carry certain information issued by the authorities or even kidnappers themselves. This presents a conundrum for journalists because there may be no way for them to independently verify the information, because the authorities and perpetrators may be deliberately including misinformation, and because the coverage itself may advance the interests of perpetrators.

Research has shown that the news coverage of kidnappings has a psychological impact not just on participants but the general public as well.[13] It obviously can increase the emotional pressure on families and friends, and can induce fright by leading the public to believe they personally face increased threats. The latter has been especially true when kidnappings involve children, provoking great fear in other parents and their children.

Journalists and news organisations thus are confronted with significant social and ethical issues when covering kidnappings in stable social settings – whether or not journalists are the victims. The questions about covering kidnappings are compounded when they take place in unstable locations and, like all coverage of kidnappings and hostage takings, require considerable thought and care.

Kidnappings in unstable locations

The challenges of covering kidnappings are compounded when kidnappings involve groups in unstable locations or settings in which active conflicts are taking place. In these locations, civil authority is weak or absent and local police and security forces are generally not able to prevent or effectively respond to kidnappings, or provide authoritative information about abductions and abductors.

The motives for the kidnapping of journalists vary widely, as discussed earlier in this book, but they are most often undertaken to punish journalists for coverage, exploit the existing chaos to abduct journalists for ransom, or bring pressure on the victim's country of origin. In some cases, abductions occur because perpetrators wish to use journalists to obtain media coverage to bring attention to their grievances, to show their effectiveness, or to instil terror.[14]

Research has found that press coverage itself does not cause acts of terrorism to occur, but that it is sometimes used by perpetrators for their purposes and can make authorities' responses to events more difficult.[15] The specific language used by the media to describe events and the ensuing tone of presentation of terroristic acts, their perpetrators, the authorities involved, and depiction of relevant policies play important roles in developing public perceptions about the perpetrators, the nature of terrorist threats, and what responses may or may not be appropriate.[16] Some violent organisations are now bypassing traditional media and using social media and other modern forms of communication to explain their cause, recruit supporters, and convey messages to their enemies.[17]

In most unstable locations, a lack of information and even misinformation about kidnappings exists because the absence of an effective local authority makes collection, verification, and dissemination of information difficult to impossible and because the uncertainties of violent conflicts regularly obscure the truth of what has happened. Because of the problems of unverified information, media covering the abductions of journalists and other parties must take great care about how they report information and avoid carrying rumours or information that mislead the public and complicate efforts to determine what has happened so that news organisations and authorities can respond effectively.

All of these issues lead governments and security forces to be wary of how they respond to the kidnappings and to be concerned with the coverage of such kidnappings, whether or not they involve journalists. Because of the uncertainties of unstable locations and the difficulties in information verification, news organisations face significant challenges when trying to cover kidnappings in such locales.

Stages and levels of media coverage of journalist kidnappings

Up to this point, this chapter has focused primarily on the challenges of covering kidnappings in general. It now turns to how kidnappings of journalists are covered – a phenomenon far less researched, but crucial for news organisations whose journalists are involved and for other news organisations reporting on kidnappings.

There are four distinct stages of media coverage of journalist kidnappings: (1) the initial disappearance or abduction stage, (2) the captivity stage, (3) the negotiation stage, and (4) the resolution stage.

The first stage is characterised by initial reports from colleagues and/ or employers that a journalist has gone missing or has been seized by some party. In distant conflict zones, employers often learn that their reporters are endangered or missing from journalists from other news organisations who are at or near the scene.

Initial reports tend to be sparse, reporting the journalist as missing, detained, or abducted, and identifying the journalists' employer or employers. They usually provide limited information about the events or which perpetrators may be involved, although sometimes reporting speculation about the captors. These initial news reports tend to be widely published and broadcast, primarily because of their salience to other reporters, editors, and news producers, but also out of the belief that bringing large-scale attention to the seizure in its immediate aftermath may lead to early release. The news organisation employing the journalist, or most visibly linked to the detained individual, may issue a statement at this stage clarifying its relationship with the journalist, acknowledging the capture, urging the release of the individual, citing the importance of the work of journalists with regard to the freedom of the press and the distribution of information that might not otherwise be possible, and asserting their independence from the governments of their countries of origin.

This pattern was illustrated when James Foley was kidnapped in 2012. GlobalPost published a story reporting his relationship with the news site, carrying a message from his father urging his release, and with his employer stating that 'Jim is a brave and dedicated reporter who has spent much of the past year covering the civil war in Syria, believing like so many of his colleagues that this is a very important story for the American people to know more about. We urge his captors to release him.'[18]

When captivity is extended beyond the initial short time frame, news coverage becomes more difficult because of the lack of new and credible information or because of the wishes of the families and employers of kidnapped journalists or their security advisers. In this stage many journalist captives tend to disappear from newspaper and broadcast media reports, but journalist safety organisations may include them in their lists of journalists missing or held hostage. The amount of and prominence of continued coverage given to kidnappings also varies widely depending upon many factors, including the proximity of the kidnapping to the relevant media, its duration, political salience, and the national journalistic cultures and accepted practices of the media making the reports.

Three levels of visibility of kidnappings have been identified by Keren Tenenboim-Weinblatt: (1) 'sustained visibility' in which media coverage is relatively constant, (2) 'delayed visibility' in which information and coverage is withheld for a time in media blackouts, and (3) 'cyclical visibility' in which coverage occurs in waves over lengthy kidnappings.[19]

Whether, and the extent to which, media cover kidnappings depends on circumstances, the wishes of the families and the employing news organisations, and the wishes of kidnappers. The coverage is also influenced by pressure brought by law enforcement and intelligence agencies and advice from security advisers to companies whose employees have been kidnapped.

'It is a difficult fence to straddle. You just do what is best for the safety of the individual involved and consider the wishes of the family', says Philip Balboni, President/CEO of GlobalPost, who twice had to deal with the kidnapping of James Foley in Libya and then Syria.[20]

Disclosure of the kidnapping and continued coverage by the media can produce benefits such as attracting new strands of information and may induce contact by kidnappers. However, such coverage may also produce false leads and contacts by people pretending to be kidnappers, and may endanger the lives of not only the kidnapped journalists but others who were kidnapped with the journalist, as well as other news media personnel working in the region, by provoking copy-cat incidents.

Media blackouts or silence tend to reduce the 'value' of the hostage to their abductors if they are using hostages as a basis for publicity. Blackouts tend to reduce the pressure on kidnappers during negotiations when many factors can scuttle contacts and discussions. Negotiations are a particularly difficult stage in captivity in which public and private messages carry great import and often lead to news blackouts being sought by perpetrators, negotiators, or media companies themselves and can lead to negotiators and media companies censoring information that might make a resolution more difficult.

During the ill-fated kidnapping of Steven Sotloff, a strict blackout was maintained in part because his employer and journalist colleagues wanted to withhold information that he was Jewish and a dual US–Israeli citizen, information that would have greatly endangered him. When photojournalist Matt Schrier, who was held with Peter Theo

Curtis but released before him, was interviewed by CBS News's *60 Minutes* in November 2013, the interview was edited to remove references to Curtis being tortured so that those facts would not further complicate negotiations.

The resolution or the end of a kidnapping is typically greeted with significant but short coverage. Following a 'good' ending in which kidnapped journalists are released, new reports tend to inform of their release, their health, and the relief and gratitude of the families and employers. Details of how the release occurred, who played a role, and ransoms paid or consideration given to such are only rarely included. When the kidnapping is not resolved successfully and the result is the death of the journalist, news reports tend to emphasise the dangerous nature of the profession and the importance of journalism to democratic society, the commitment of the journalist to the profession, and the grief of family, friends, and employers.

When Ghislaine Dupont and Claude Verlon of Radio France Internationale were kidnapped and killed in Mali, for example, the Associated Press reported their kidnapping and deaths, and reactions of colleagues. It reported an RFI statement saying Dupont was 'passionate about her job and the African continent that she covered since joining RFI' and that Verlon was 'used to difficult terrain throughout the world'.[21] The BBC used their story on the killings to tell readers 'Their deaths bring to 42 the number of journalists around the world killed so far in 2013'.[22]

Following the resolution of a kidnapping, more information about the events and perpetrators may become available and may be reported. Follow-up stories may tell the story of what happened and why. Such was the case with the release of freelance journalist Michael Scott Moore, who was released in Somalia in 2004 after two years in captivity. A CNN report carried news that Moore had been writing on how European fishing activities were driving Somali fisherman to piracy when captured and who he had been writing for. The report also stated that his employing news organisation had not covered the kidnapping on the recommendation of the FBI and State Department, that the release was negotiated by tribal elders, and that gaining freedom after a kidnapping in the region almost always occurred after payment of ransom, although no one would comment on whether a ransom was paid for Moore's release.[23]

Richard Engel, a foreign correspondent for NBC television, and his colleagues were kidnapped in Syria in 2012 before being rescued by a rival group of the kidnappers. After his release, Engel reported that his captors indicated they were Shi'ite militiamen aligned with the government of Bashar Assad and that he had been rescued by a Sunni group affiliated with the Free Syrian Army opposed to Assad. However, truth can be elusive and it was ultimately determined that he was actually held by the group that later reportedly rescued him.[24]

Journalists and news organisations reporting kidnappings thus have to be aware that the information they receive may be inaccurate, erroneous, or be designed to serve the purposes of governments or combatants. Thus great care must be taken in reporting all stages of kidnappings to avoid misleading readers, listeners, and viewers or playing into the hands of interested parties.

Ethical questions arising from journalist kidnappings

How news organisations and journalists respond to and cover kidnappings involves ethical questions that require greater transparency and debate within the journalistic community. The answers to these questions are not clear-cut but involve the complex balancing of issues of safety with those of credibility, accuracy, fairness, and the basic functions of journalism.

Reporting with bodyguards

Journalists around the world have long had adversarial relationships with security guards for political figures and celebrities who have attempted to keep reporters away from their clients. However, journalists are increasingly turning to bodyguards to protect them against drug cartels and other criminal gangs, corrupt political figures, and the risks of reporting in conflict zones. The issues of using armed guards or arming journalists themselves are not often discussed publicly, but news organisations' decisions on how to protect their reporters must include examination of such issues. There are significant ethical issues involved in the trade-off between journalists' safety and their ability to continue covering certain stories and locations.

Although individual journalists working in high-risk areas are rarely protected by bodyguards, larger international news organisations began employing them in locations of extreme danger about a decade ago. Both CNN and the BBC have occasionally provided armed bodyguards to accompany news crews into areas they deemed extremely dangerous. Some journalists object to such security, believing it makes it more difficult for them to interact with the public and sources, by calling further attention to them, and escalates the danger they face because they may be mistaken for combatants.

Most journalists will not carry weapons themselves because it is seen as undermining their position as observers and can lead to mistaken identification as combatants or spies, but some argue there are occasions when it is justified.[25] Some news organisations forbid their employees from carrying weapons. 'Reporters, photographers and other editorial personnel on assignment from the *Times* to cover a war or civil conflict must never carry a weapon, openly or concealed on their person or in their vehicle', according to the *New York Times* policy. '[T]he newspaper believes it is imperative that they be perceived always as neutral observers. The carrying of a weapon, for whatever reason, jeopardizes a journalist's status as a neutral.'[26]

That view is not universally held, however, particularly by journalists and news organisations under threat in places such as Pakistan, the Philippines, Colombia, and Mexico, where violence against journalists has been endemic, views on gun ownership differ, and some journalists are willing to carry weapons for self-protection.[27] In locations where attacks on journalists are frequent, it is not unusual for journalists to travel with armed guards and have their offices and homes protected by them too.

These practices raise ethical questions about the extent to which news organisations should support reporting done under the watchful eyes of armed guards and by journalists arming themselves. These may create issues of trust with those interviewed, alter the information journalists convey in their report, and create credibility issues with sources and audiences.

Ethical questions involving coverage of kidnappings

The coverage of kidnapping and hostage taking raises numerous issues unique to each case, but there are shared primary ethical considerations relating to the style in which the kidnapping is covered, the extent of coverage, and what information is included in news reports. Of particular concern is whether the information conveyed will increase the risk of harm to hostages, whether the information will be useful to perpetrators, and if it will unfavourably affect the response of authorities.

The Canadian Broadcasting Corporation's guidelines for covering kidnapping and hostage taking encompasses these ethical issues by asserting that the two primary principles of coverage should be careful adherence to the journalistic purpose for coverage and minimising harm. The guidelines build upon its Journalistic Standards and Practices statement, which stipulates 'CBC journalists must ensure that any action they take will not further endanger the lives of the hostages or interfere with efforts of authorities to secure the hostages' release. They must guard against being used or manipulated by the terrorists/hostage takers.'[28]

Determining what information to convey or withhold is always complex in kidnapping and hostage situations, but the ethical issues become particularly thorny when journalists are involved, because the self-interest of journalists as a professional group to protect one of their own and of news organisations to protect employees become involved. Other news organisations and journalists must carefully consider their willingness to acquiesce to those interests.

Coverage and news blackouts involving journalist kidnappings have led to deep criticism and concern because of the control of information and the framing of stories by news organisations whose journalists are involved, and choices made about coverage of abductions of personnel from other news providers. The debate has focused on the obligations of journalists to inform in a timely and accurate fashion, why journalists are more likely to report on journalist kidnappings than those involving other individuals who make up the majority of kidnapping victims, and why news organisations tend to be more willing to withhold information when journalists are involved rather than other types of victims.

Whether journalists should withhold information or pursue blackouts has been hotly contested in journalism circles, with widely disparate views on news organisations agreeing to withhold information or deliberately providing incomplete information.[29] It is, of course, easier to debate the issue in the abstract than to have to make a decision about disclosure when directly involved in a kidnapping. But non-disclosure can create harm to others.

A particularly significant endangerment problem resulting from media blackouts emerged in 2013 when more than a dozen cases of journalist kidnappings in Syria were kept secret, not just from the public but other journalists and news organisations as well. Although it recognised that there can be benefits in keeping quiet, especially during negotiations, the Committee to Protect Journalists ultimately felt it needed to warn other journalists about how dangerous Syria had become. It released the total number of kidnappings there without releasing victims' names and information about their personal circumstances. 'Blackouts can have an unintended consequence of camouflaging the actual dangers of the situation', Rob Mahoney, the CPJ's deputy director, said when releasing the data. 'It was in the interest of everyone that the scale of the problem be demonstrated.'[30]

Other ethical considerations have been raised involving the coverage of kidnappings that end in the death of journalists, especially when the intention of kidnappers is to shock the world by showing the executions of those they have detained, such as Steven Sotloff and James Foley. Many news organisations debated how they would use video and photos of the executions, with most showing the scene but not the moment of killing; others, however, carried more explicit visuals. Central to the decisions made were cultural and company values about decency, privacy at the moment of death, and effects on the family, colleagues, and the public.

Coverage of journalist kidnappings thus creates significant ethical concerns about which editors and journalists need to be cognisant and which should be employed to inform their discussions and decisions about how to cover kidnappings. There are no simple answers to the ethical questions, and decisions must be made carefully by individual news organisations.

In determining how to cover the kidnapping of journalists, editors need to carefully consider why and how they are covering the kidnappings. This involves deliberately considering the following questions. Should the coverage of foreign kidnappings differ from the coverage of domestic kidnappings? Should the kidnapping of a journalist gain more coverage or prominence than that given to a kidnapping of other individuals? Should the coverage of a member of your own staff or your freelancer differ from coverage of those from other news organisations? How does a media blackout affect public understanding and other journalists' perceptions of risks? If coverage is constrained, how will you explain it to your audience during and after the kidnapping?

Answering these ethical questions involves issues of safety, equity, and justice, and the credibility effects of leaving the public uninformed or misleading them. Because of the rapid decisions and high stress that occur during a kidnapping, debates on these issues should take place well before they occur as part of organisational preparedness and contingency planning.

6

The Roles of Journalist Safety Organisations

News organisations are not left to tackle the challenges of preparation and increasing journalist safety on their own. A number of highly visible international organisations focus on issues of journalist safety and training of news media personnel to better understand the risks they face. Such training can potentially help them avoid kidnap or at the very least better understand how they might react if they find themselves in such a situation. These organisations are good sources of information regarding how kidnappings evolve and often transpire and they also often have connections with journalists who have been through similar situations. Some also play an important role in advocating for the release of hostages when journalists are detained. Direct resolution of kidnappings is not in their mandate, however, so they must be regarded as ancillary to that task.

Consequently, these media associations and journalist safety organisations tend not to be major players in individual kidnapping cases because after the hostage taking they can only document and denounce attacks on journalists and advocate for governmental and intergovernmental protection. The World Association of Newspapers and News Publishers (WAN-IFRA), for example, could do little more than denounce the beheading of Steven Sotloff in September 2014. Its Secretary General Larry Kilman issued a press release, saying: 'We are appalled by the gruesome murder of Steven Sotloff. ... The international community must do its utmost to ensure that journalism and journalists are respected and the perpetrators of these crimes are brought to justice.'[1]

Although journalist and media organisations are usually not highly involved during a kidnapping itself, journalist safety organisations play important roles in making news organisations and journalists aware of risk levels. A number of organisations offer hostile environment training to prepare journalists to evaluate the environments of locations from which they will report, become aware of dangers, and initiate practices designed to improve their safety. Some also provide training on journalist safety challenges found in particular countries, regions, or conflict zones. Others offer additional training in first aid that helps journalists deal with injuries to colleagues in the field and to improve digital communication safety to reduce risks of being tracked or losing sensitive information if detained (a list of resources for such training is found in Appendix 1).

Many news organisations have long had safety guidelines for their own employees, but the growing reliance on freelancers working in conflict zones on behalf of major media led to a coalition of journalist safety organisations and large media organisations – including the Associated Press, Reuters, Agence France-Presse, the BBC, PBS, Frontline, and Bloomberg – to establish safety standards in February 2015 (see Appendix 1). 'There has been an ongoing debate about freelance journalists going into high-risk regions without the support afforded to full-time staffers. Many lack the basics, such as insurance, proper protective gear, security advisors and support from the media outlets they serve', said the International Center for Journalists, one of the standards' sponsors.[2]

Freelancers and organisations associated with them have long advocated for better protection and support in conflict zones. The Frontline Club for journalists was established in London to help pursue those purposes, recognising the unique needs of reporters and their fixers in areas embroiled in conflict. It has long advocated for better support from news organisations and conducts safety training and digital updates through its freelance registry.

Most safety organisations and training programmes for journalists are based in larger Western nations, but provide services to journalists worldwide through networks of journalists and press freedom organisations and online activities. Reporters Sans Frontières, for example, has links with local organisations and journalists in 150 countries.

Global safety principles and practices endorsed by major journalist safety and news organisations

For journalists on dangerous assignments

- Before setting out on any assignment in a conflict zone or any dangerous environment, journalists should have basic skills to care for themselves or injured colleagues.

- All journalists are encouraged to complete a recognised news industry first-aid course, to carry a suitable first-aid kit, and continue their training to stay up-to-date on standards of care and safety, both physical and psychological. Before undertaking an assignment in such zones, journalists should seek adequate medical insurance covering them in a conflict zone or area of infectious disease.
- Journalists in active war zones should be aware of the need and importance of having protective ballistic clothing, including armoured jackets and helmets. Journalists operating in a conflict zone or dangerous environment should endeavour to complete an industry-recognised hostile environment course.
- Journalists should work with colleagues on the ground and with news organisations to complete a careful risk assessment before travelling to any hostile or dangerous environment and measure the journalistic value of an assignment against the risks.
- On assignment, journalists should plan and prepare in detail how they will operate, including identifying routes, transport, contacts, and a communications strategy with daily check-in routines with a colleague in the region or their editor. Whenever practical, journalists should take appropriate precautions to secure mobile and internet communications from intrusion and tracking.
- Journalists should work closely with their news organisations, the organisation that has commissioned them, or their colleagues in the industry if acting independently, to understand the risks of any specific assignment. In doing so, they should seek and take into account the safety information and travel advice of professional colleagues, local contacts, embassies, and security personnel. And, likewise, they should share safety information with colleagues to help prevent them harm.
- Journalists should leave next of kin details with news organisations, ensuring that these named contacts have clear instructions and action plans in the case of injury, kidnap, or death in the field.

For news organisations making assignments in dangerous places

- Editors and news organisations recognise that local journalists and freelancers, including photographers and videographers, play an increasingly vital role in international coverage, particularly on dangerous stories.
- Editors and news organisations should show the same concern for the welfare of local journalists and freelancers that they do for staffers.
- News organisations and editors should endeavour to treat journalists and freelancers they use on a regular basis in a similar manner to the way they treat staffers when it comes to issues of safety training, first aid, and other safety equipment, and responsibility in the event of injury or kidnap.
- Editors and news organisations should be aware of, and factor in, the additional costs of training, insurance, and safety equipment in war zones. They should clearly delineate before an assignment what a freelancer will be paid and what expenses will be covered.
- Editors and news organisations should recognise the importance of prompt payment for freelancers. When setting assignments, news organisations should endeavour to provide agreed-upon expenses in advance, or as soon as possible on completion of work, and pay for work done in as timely a manner as possible.
- Editors and news organisations should ensure that all freelance journalists are given fair recognition in bylines and credits for the work they do both at the time the work is published or broadcast and if it is later submitted for awards, unless the news organisation and the freelancer agree that crediting the journalist can compromise the safety of the freelancer and/or the freelancer's family.
- News organisations should not make an assignment with a freelancer in a conflict zone or dangerous environment unless the news organisation is prepared to take the same responsibility for the freelancer's wellbeing in the event of kidnap or injury as

> it would a staffer. News organisations have a moral responsibility to support journalists to whom they give assignments in dangerous areas, as long as the freelancer complies with the rules and instructions of the news organisation.

Who works to protect journalists?

The most important journalist safety organisations working to protect journalists are the Committee to Protect Journalists (CPJ), Reporters Sans Frontières (RSF), the International News Safety Institute (INSI), and the Dart Center for Journalism and Trauma.

Committee to Protect Journalists, www.cpj.org

The Committee to Protect Journalists (CPJ) describes itself as 'an independent, non-profit organization that promotes press freedom worldwide'. Based in New York, it handles hundreds of cases every year of journalists who are in danger around the world and has a network of regional coordinators. The CPJ exists to 'ensure that journalists everywhere are able to do their job freely', says Executive Director Joel Simon, specifically those 'individual journalists who put their lives and liberty on the line to report the news', and to ensure they know that they 'have the support of colleagues around the world when governments respond with violence and pressure'.[3]

The vast majority of the journalists whom the CPJ defends are local journalists. They are considerably more vulnerable than their international colleagues who have the protective benefit of much higher visibility. Simon says the CPJ tries to give these local journalists the same level of visibility as their international counterparts. When it becomes aware of cases of journalists who are in danger of death, arrest, or detention, the CPJ notifies its worldwide network of media, which serves to alert the governments or authorities in the country where the journalist is at risk that there is an international outcry. It also provides a strong element of solidarity from the journalism community for the affected individual or individuals.

Since it was set up over three decades ago, the CPJ has grown into a global organisation with a full-time headquarters staff plus regional coordinators around the world. It has sent more than 100 delegations to dozens of nations to investigate abuses, detail the status of press freedom, present evidence to leading officials, and publicise the plight of journalists. Its Executive Board includes leading advocates of press freedom and high-profile journalists and media executives including Terry Anderson, the former Associated Press correspondent who was held hostage in Lebanon for seven years, CNN anchor Christiane Amanpour, Arianna Huffington of the Huffington Post, and Jonathan Klein, the CPJ's co-founder and CEO of the global digital media company Getty Images.

In recent years, the CPJ has launched an internet advocacy plan, specifically focused on protecting the growing number of online journalists. It also has a Journalist Assistance programme which was launched in 2001 to provide emergency and long-term assistance to those in dire need. 'When it started 10 years ago, the Committee to Protect Journalists' assistance program was tiny, helping just a handful of journalists. Today it's a huge part of our work and we assist more than 200 journalists and their families each year. This growth tracks the surge in the numbers of journalists at-risk around the world', says CPJ Deputy Director Robert Mahoney.

> Technology has enabled many more people to gather and publish news but authoritarian governments and militias do not welcome the spotlight. And for some groups reporters are not observers but targets to be silenced or exploited for propaganda or ransom. In the last five years, especially since the upheaval in the Middle East, hundreds of journalists have been forced to flee. Our Journalist Assistance program has helped 452 journalists in exile over that period, and 82 in just this year alone.[4]

Like the other media support groups detailed below, the CPJ records the number of journalists who are killed every year, of whom it says approximately 90 per cent are murdered. The CPJ operates on an annual budget of about £2.8 million ($4.5 million) and employs 38 staff members.

Reporters Sans Frontières, http://en.rsf.org

Reporters Sans Frontières (RSF) is a Paris-based non-profit organisation with a mandate to work in the area of press freedom and to support journalists who are in danger. RSF monitors and denounces attacks on press freedom around the world, issuing more than 1,000 press releases per year on violations of the freedom of information. It acts in cooperation with governments to fight censorship and laws aimed at restricting the freedom of information.

In addition, RSF provides moral and financial assistance to journalists who are persecuted and their families. The organisation also offers material assistance to 'war correspondents' to enhance their safety. It 'has been working for decades all over the world with the families, employers and governments of journalists missing, imprisoned or held hostage to provide on-the-ground information and contacts, media strategy advice, platforms for the support committees and any logistic assistance needed according to each specific case,' says Delphine Halgand, Director of the Washington DC office. One example of their work is that RSF has been assisting and advising the family of Austin Tice since his kidnapping in August 2012 and developed and implemented the #FreeAustinTice campaign starting in February 2015.

Established 30 years ago, RSF now has a worldwide presence with correspondents in 150 countries. It issues an annual list of 'predators of press freedom' as well as 'heroes', collates information about the number of journalists killed in the course of their work and frequently responds to the arrest, detention, and kidnapping of journalists by calling for their release and urging its extensive network to put pressure on governments and authorities to do so. It operates on a budget of approximately £2.9 million (€4 million) annually.

International News Safety Institute, www.newssafety.org

The International News Safety Institute (INSI) is a London-based non-profit organisation that provides safety advice and training to journalists working in difficult and dangerous places around the world.

The INSI was founded by the International Press Institute and the International Federation of Journalists in 2003, providing a strong message that journalist safety is the domain of both employers and employees. It has successfully established itself as the safety body for the whole news industry.

Today its members include some of the world's leading news organisations, including CNN, the BBC, and Reuters. Their membership donations provide the INSI's core costs while it raises funds for training from governmental and non-governmental organisations such as UNESCO and the foreign ministries of various countries. The training it provides is predominantly for local journalists who are not able to rely on the support of major news organisations to pay for them to learn about safety measures and equipment. It covers a wide range of subjects ranging from conflict to civil unrest and natural disasters. The INSI has provided training to approximately 2,000 journalists in dozens of countries since its launch and has recently piloted safety training by female trainers for women journalists.

'The risks to free speech and independent journalism are greater than ever – from murder, violent intimidation, kidnap, censorship and more', says INSI chairman Richard Sambrook. 'The work of INSI makes a practical difference to many hundreds of otherwise vulnerable journalists around the world in understanding and managing the risks they face.'[5]

The INSI also coordinates an information exchange between its members during breaking news stories such as the Arab uprisings, where organisations often need to make decisions based on time-sensitive information. It publishes information and advisories for news media workers heading into challenging environments to enable them to better understand the risks they face.

Instrumental in the passage of UN Resolution 1738 on the protection of journalists, the INSI also played a lead role in the development of the Green Book, which sets out the relationship between the media and the military. It has also published a number of books including *Dying to Tell the Story*, about the journalists who died during the first months of the Iraq War in 2003, and *No Woman's Land: On the Frontlines with Female Reporters*, the first book dedicated to the safety of women journalists.

'INSI's focus on the role of women journalists is crucial. On the front lines of today's conflicts, a growing number of journalists, both foreign and local, are female', says BBC Chief International Correspondent

Lyse Doucet. 'They have particular concerns and challenges and also form part of the global community of journalists who face unprecedented risks in telling the stories that matter.'[6] Female journalists face all the risks of male counterparts, but also higher risks of sexual harassment, rape, and other sexual assault. They are often wary of discussing these risks or actual incidents of assault with editors and others in the workplace for fear they will lose assignments.[7]

The INSI has worked with news organisations to put pressure on governments to release detained journalists and has created a network of experts to help support those who are dealing with kidnappings. Like the CPJ and RSF, it collates the figures of those killed. The INSI also includes media support staff as well as journalists and issues a bi-annual report called 'Killing the Messenger'.

The INSI has a core staff of two and a cadre of trainers who deliver its training, and works with a number of consultants for specialist activities and expert research. Its board includes senior news executives from organisations such as NHK, the BBC, CNN, Reuters, Globo, and the International Press Institute.

The Dart Center for Journalism and Trauma, www.dartcenter.org

 DART CENTER FOR JOURNALISM & TRAUMA
THE JOURNALISM SCHOOL AT COLUMBIA UNIVERSITY

The Dart Center for Journalism and Trauma, established in 1999, is a project of Columbia University Graduate School of Journalism, dedicated to 'informed and ethical news reporting on violence, conflict and tragedy'. Based in New York City and with satellite offices in London and Melbourne, the Dart Center provides journalists with training and resources to allow them to report effectively and professionally on stories and issues where people have experienced trauma.

The Dart Center works with a wide network of experts including mental health clinicians and trauma researchers, media experts and teachers to ensure that journalists have the skills, knowledge, and support to report sensitively in these areas and to understand their own vulnerability from exposure to trauma.

The Dart Center provides advice to journalists on how to deal with trauma and interviews those who have experienced trauma. As such, it is well-placed to provide guidance to those who may have been through kidnappings in person, or their colleagues and perhaps family members. Its director Bruce Shapiro says:

> We can measure success with the number of journalists who have participated in our programs (thousands) or the calibre of news and scientific organisations with whom we've worked as partners and collaborators (the BBC, The ABC, the Nieman Foundation, the International Society for Traumatic Stress Studies, for instance).[8]
>
> But the best metrics are on the one hand the extent of thoughtful in-depth reporting on issues such as combat veterans, refugees, sexual assault and other formerly-rare topics; and on the other, the number of news organisations which now provide some kind of trauma awareness, peer support or management trauma training for their staff.

The Center's major ongoing programmes include the annual Ochberg Fellowship seminar for journalists around the world. Bruce Shapiro says that it has played an important leadership role in two areas.

> We've helped change the culture of journalism worldwide when it comes to reporting on deeply traumatized individuals, families and communities, We also created the first newsroom trauma-awareness and peer support programs, sponsored some of the earliest research identifying psychological research as an occupational health hazard in news rooms, and are a go-to resource for news organisations and news safety advocates concerned about colleagues who experience severe trauma and threat.[9]

The Dart Center was established with a $7 million gift from the Dart Foundation and has a core staff of four persons.

Roles played by media support organisations in helping to prevent and end kidnappings

The main roles these media support groups play in the field of kidnappings are four-fold: providing training to mitigate safety risks, sharing information, lobbying, and providing assistance afterwards to the journalists directly involved and their colleagues who may have been affected indirectly by the experience.

Organisations such as the INSI provide safety training that works on a preventative agenda, helping journalists to better understand the risks they face and to adopt skills to mitigate those risks. The INSI's training includes a focus on getting journalists to undertake effective preparation, research, and planning ahead of stories, to be aware of what measures they should take to ensure their personal safety is not compromised by understanding the environments in which they are working and who might want to target them in those environments, and to understand how and when to take steps to ensure that their routes and routines, bases and transport choices do not make them more vulnerable to attack.

The training helps journalists prepare to cover the story by learning how to assess risks and take any necessary steps to mitigate them. It helps journalists understand the importance of having a reliable plan in place in case of kidnap, so their news organisations know where to start looking for them.

The training also provides information about the kind of kit and equipment, such as trackers, to consider using to help journalists if they find themselves in difficulty. The INSI works with individuals and organisations to have a contingency plan in place if things do go wrong and provides training for its members and non-members on how to manage a crisis. Some of this advice is available on its website.

INSI board member and Globo executive Marcelo Moreira notes the importance of safety training as much from the preventative side as anything else: 'When no one dies, organisations forget about safety training.'[10]

INSI safety and security adviser Caroline Neil says training is vital if you work in a hostile environment: 'You don't want to be in the middle of nowhere with your driver or colleague bleeding out after a car crash, only to realise you don't know how to save their life and wondering why you never found the time to take a medical refresher.'[11]

From an information-sharing perspective, the CPJ, RSF, and the INSI all can and do play an active role through their extensive and well-established networks when journalists are kidnapped, although obviously their regional strengths may differ. They may be party to media blackouts. They may be called on to try to ascertain when and where individuals were last seen, or whom they were meeting if the journalist has not left that information with their newsroom or a trusted contact, which may be more likely if they are a freelancer. However, the CPJ's Simon says that media blackouts disguise the depth of the problem. In an article for the *Columbia Journalism Review* in September 2014, he explained:

In Syria, approximately 30 journalists were reported missing at the end of 2013. Blackouts may have made sense in some individual cases, but collectively the large number of them obscured the scope of the problem and reduced media coverage of the troubling shift in the security environment: The Islamic State was actively hunting for journalists to abduct. In order to draw attention to the risk, CPJ decided to make public the total number of kidnapped journalists in Syria without providing names or details of specific cases.[12]

In 2008, the INSI launched a global hostage crisis help centre for journalists and other news professionals kidnapped as a result of their work. The Dart Center was one of the organisations which supported this. The service offered a point of contact and free advice for news organisations and individuals confronted by a colleague's kidnap, and was also supported by major news outlets such as CNN and the BBC, media support groups such as the Rory Peck Trust and journalists who had themselves been through a kidnapping such as the BBC's Alan Johnston and the *LA Times*'s Tina Susman. However, the INSI made it clear that it would not attempt to resolve specific hostage situations or act as an intermediary in negotiations.

'It was a great idea, enthusiastically supported by our members and a hit at News Xchange – but no one actually used it as far as I know. It's quite possible, given the high confidentiality of these issues, that the network may have been used without our involvement, but I can't be sure', said Rodney Pinder, Director of the INSI at the time, adding that the fact that the service was for organisations which were experiencing kidnap for the first time might have explained the poor take-up of the service.[13]

In addition to often sensitive information sharing, the CPJ and RSF play a key role in advocacy, putting pressure on governments and authorities to take any steps they can to help secure the release of journalists, highlighting the depth of the problem where they can and where there are no media blackouts in place, and keeping a record of the numbers of journalists kidnapped around the world.

How training aims to improve safety

Safety training focuses on preparing journalists to better understand and mitigate the risks they face wherever and whenever they are doing their jobs.

Many news organisations classify locations based on how 'hostile' they are and will require those working for them in such environments to undertake pre-deployment training. This is often known as hostile environment and first-aid training, although there are variations on this name. It usually takes the form of a four-to-five-day course for those who have not completed any similar training and then a two-to-three-day 'refresher' every three years.

As well as preparing these individuals to better deal with difficult and dangerous situations, such training also allows the organisations the journalists work for to show that they take seriously their duty to care for their employees and those contracted to work for them. For individuals and organisations, it is also an important element of any pre-deployment risk assessment that may be needed as a reference if the individual is injured, kidnapped, or harmed and may ultimately be used in legal cases.

'Risk assessing is part of the planning framework prior to deployment. We use the document as a useful planning tool for staff and deploying managers to think through the implications of the deployments, identify potential risks and articulate how they can be managed safely', says a senior person at the BBC, who asked not to be named.[14] Such risk assessments help identify the kinds of training that will be appropriate.

Comprehensive safety training for journalists dates back more than two decades and began after the proliferation of the 24-hour news channels and the conflict in the Balkans. The number of training providers remained relatively stable for a number of years, but since the start of the uprisings across the Middle East and North Africa, there has been a manifold increase. There are now dozens of organisations offering some kind of training for journalists. There are numerous reasons for this, two of which are an increase in the number of soldiers leaving the military after the conflicts in Iraq and Afghanistan, and the realisation that it is a lucrative market in which to work – some courses cost upwards of £2,000 per participant for a five-day course, which includes board and lodging.

Surprisingly, given the importance afforded to the training by the news industry, there is currently no regulatory body validating, or providing an overview of, this training and the market within which it exists, unlike in the related private security industry which is regulated by the Security Industry Authority in the UK. Nor is there any consistency in terms of the delivery, the content, the quality, and the duration of these courses, although the INSI is working with its partners to try to establish an agreed list of content relevant to the safety of journalists that should form part of any reputable training.

The BBC has often been regarded as providing the *de facto* standard for safety training. It was the first to opt for the five-day course, but it could be argued that this was more random than a reflection of the absolute needs of the news industry as a whole. The BBC was able to do this in part because it has the financial and personnel resources necessary, entered safety training early, has an influence on global journalism practice, and such a large number of journalists go through its courses. The broadcaster has its own training provider, which has caused some challenges for freelancers approaching the BBC for work if they have undergone training with another provider, which the BBC does not recognise.

On these training courses, varying weight is afforded to different subjects and diverse training methods are used, sometimes because of the expertise of the providers or the demands of specific news organisations. Although it is important for training providers to offer content that fits the size of the programme and objectives they want to achieve, the need for some standardisation and recognition of training from multiple providers is apparent.

In most courses the following subjects are likely to be taught, using both practical scenarios and classroom-based learning and activities: planning and preparation (documentation, planning, equipment, communications), risk identification and assessment, personal security, basic first aid (including primary and secondary survey), weapons awareness and reaction to gunfire, civil unrest and crowds, bleeding, shock and head injuries, crisis management, and trauma. Other subjects may include detecting and escaping from minefields, check points, road and vehicle safety, and more advanced first aid, as well as advice on how to stay safe in extreme environments (i.e. cold, heat, or after environmental disasters).

All of the content needs to be relevant to the individual's experience and background and taught by highly knowledgeable trainers with experience in conflict zones. The training also needs to take into account the limitations of the resources, equipment, and access, for instance, to communications networks or emergency services, that journalists may experience when they are in the hostile environment.

With regard to kidnapping as a specific subject in these courses, some – but not all – providers will include it as a classroom-based lesson; others will include kidnap scenarios in their training.

Some will include an ambush scenario, in which participants on the course are stopped, forced out of their cars, robbed, and left on the side of the road, often blindfolded. Such a scenario will allow those attending the course to manage their shock and fear, without forcing them to stand masked or blindfolded in stress positions where they may be interrogated for an extended period of time. However, other training organisations involve both scenarios, with the former ambush usually preceding a mock kidnapping.

Simon Marr, Director of Safety, Security and Resilience at the BBC, says that the key thing for him is

exposing people to some of the raw emotions that they might experience to prepare them for the 'shock of capture', and allowing them to work out if it is something they are prepared or willing to experience in the future. It's also about trying to give them some tools for dealing with the experience so they can survive the ordeal with as much dignity as possible.[15]

Many of the aspects that precede a kidnapping are covered in the training and hence the risk may be lowered by a focus on personal safety, preparation, risk assessment, communications plans, and also by an understanding of what contingency measures to take. The emotional stress that may be associated with a kidnapping is also likely to be handled in sessions on trauma, which are widely covered by training providers.

In addition to field and foreign journalists, some of the larger news organisations do send their managers and news executives on this course. It is extremely important that those who hold the purse strings and are responsible for the decision-making and deployments are able to make informed decisions when asking their colleagues to work in dangerous and difficult environments. However, it would also be helpful if those on the news desk were also more aware of some of the pressures and risks that their colleagues face because they may be the first point of contact if the overseas journalists find themselves in a stressful situation. However, the issue of money and the difficulty of juggling busy work schedules often restrict this.

Some news organisations will also pay for commissioned freelancers to go on these courses or they may rely on those who have previously undergone training to go to difficult places. Unfortunately, not all organisations do this. The reality may be different when a story breaks, particularly if this coincides with spiralling deployment costs either on the present or concurrent stories, or if the news organisation does not have its 'own' people in a place where they can be deployed to the location of the story.

'The question of whether news organisations should be commissioning freelance journalists to operate in war zones has become especially pertinent in recent years', says Ruth Sherlock, the Middle East Correspondent for the *Telegraph*.

> *The answers found to this problem are often absolute, black or white: some organisations have put a blanket ban on using freelancers, no matter how experienced they are. Others take copy from the journalists, without asking questions about their safety in the war zone, or offering to pay their expenses, thereby causing the journalist to often take huge risks to operate in a dangerous environment cheaply. Neither of these are good options in an age where fewer and fewer journalists are staff, and more and more excellent and experienced reporters are making the decision to operate on a freelance basis.*[16]

'The solution is flexibility: companies can use a freelance journalist if the person is known to people inside the organisation as someone who is sensible in such environments', she says, adding that the company should cover all necessities in a war zone: a driver, translator, satellite phone, safety equipment, etc. 'When an organisation does hire the freelancers, that journalist should be afforded the same benefits as a staff reporter for the time they are contracted.' Despite this noble view of news organisations' responsibilities and obligations, few media employing freelancers provide that level of support.

A number of journalists working for independent production companies commissioned by large media organisations reportedly go to extremely dangerous locations with minimal training because of cost cutting or because, with the knee-jerk reaction to 'breaking news' in danger zones and conflicts, there is simply not enough time to have people take these courses. There is a sense that a little training and warnings are better than nothing if full training cannot be provided.

Among some of the more recent entrants to the news industry, there is also a sense that training is not necessary. This may be a question of either the cultural importance of safety or the simple fact that many major news organisations only really become aware of safety issues after they have lost one of their colleagues and these new organisations have not yet experienced that. It is important that the entire industry subscribes to a greater duty of care and commitment to provide training and equipment and that individuals and organisations understand that both have a responsibility to ensure they are as prepared as they possibly can be for the risks they may face.

There is a growing debate as to whether the world is getting more dangerous for freelance journalists. One of the key arguments hangs on the access to training. Although they may not historically have had such, freelancers are able to access safety training quite readily today. Some will continue to argue that the costs are restrictive; however, much of what is offered to freelancers is available at a reduced rate.

Organisations like the Rory Peck Trust provide bursaries for freelancers to attend safety training courses. RISC (Reporters Instructed in Saving Colleagues) provides free first-aid training and other organisations such as the INSI and providers such as UK-based Remote Trauma, working in conjunction with the Frontline Club, have offered training either for free or at cost. In addition, the INSI has provided safety training overseas for free and that is often open to freelancers, while RSF is also able to help freelancers with insurance and equipment.

7

Good Practices for Journalists and their Employers

How the journalistic community responds to the threat of journalist kidnapping is crucial to both the safety of journalists and ensuring that dangerous conflict zones receive needed coverage. The response cannot merely be statements of outrage and demands for more safety for journalists, but requires clear analysis and specific action by news organisations and journalists themselves to look after the well-being of journalists dispatched to conflict zones.

Employers are morally responsible for the security of the employees and freelancers that they oversee and must provide them with the training and other support required for them to operate safely in hostile environments. They are legally responsible for employees, but generally have lower legal responsibility for freelancers. Simultaneously, journalists are also responsible for exercising caution and protecting themselves and should try to defend their employers from harm that may result from the choices they make during the course of their work. Both must work jointly to increase safety in the field. The costs of training and safe practices pale by comparison to the costs of responding to kidnappings and the emotional toll they take on those kidnapped, their families, loved ones, and friends.

Some news organisations have chosen to avoid all those risks and costs by exercising extreme caution and ceasing deployments of journalists to dangerous locations. This reduces their ability to gather news and information in conflict zones, affecting their ability to meet the public's need for information about events and developments in the world. News organisations that choose this course of action have professional obligations to their audiences to explicitly develop and employ other means for gathering that news and information and inform their viewers, listeners, and readers why they are doing so.

Although the moral and ethical considerations for news organisations to protect journalists are apparent, the abilities of news providers worldwide to address them effectively vary significantly because of unequal resources and the disparate institutional realities under which they operate. Journalists working for larger news firms in wealthier countries are afforded greater safety support and protection than are journalists from poorer countries and news organisations with fewer financial resources. Because of the global development disparities, journalists from the Southern Hemisphere thus tend to have less support than those from the Northern Hemisphere. Concurrently, news organisations everywhere tend to provide greater support for their employees than for freelancers, creating an institutional inequality amongst journalists.

The increasing reliance of news organisations on freelancers in conflict areas has made those journalists particularly vulnerable because many do not have the organisational support of employed journalists and many lack sufficient risk and safety training. A recent industry-wide survey found that 79 per cent believed freelancers faced a bigger threat of kidnapping today than a decade ago.[1] Nevertheless, some freelancers feel that economic and professional necessity forces them to take risks in pursuit of stories. When hiring freelancers to provide coverage, news organisations have moral obligations to consider their safety and should comply with the global safety principles and practices set out in Chapter 6.

News executives and frontline journalists for the most part agree that the most high-profile threat to the safety of journalists in recent years is the kidnapping of journalists in Syria by the terror group ISIS for ransom, propaganda, and theatre purposes. Nakhle El Hage, the director of news and current affairs at Al Arabiya television, says that kidnapping is 'a powerful tool intended to drain the energy of news agencies'.[2] Kevin Sutcliffe, the head of EU news programming at VICE News, says this recent development on the part of ISIS and gangs in Syria is simply opportunistic gangsterism: 'In places like Syria you are moving across territories controlled by a number of groups. This patchwork is harder to understand. Who hates who is complicated, and you can't say who controls this patch of land. It's more chaotic now.'[3]

The heavy focus on the large number of kidnappings in Syria and Iraq, however, masks the fact that abductions are taking place worldwide and that the threat must be perceived in all conflict zones and locations where local authority is weak and hazards are heightened. News organisations worldwide need be cognisant of and respond to the domestic and regional kidnapping threats they face – whether in Eastern Europe, Latin America, Asia, or elsewhere.

The challenges of kidnappings require news organisations to individually prepare themselves and their journalists for operations in hostile environments, set limits on risks, and be prepared for the possibility of kidnapping. The journalistic community as a whole needs to more directly address the threats and improve the ways media organisations respond to incidents to help reduce the number of abductions and improve the effectiveness of responses to them.

Two key findings emerge from the review of the issues surrounding kidnappings and the experiences reviewed in this study: (1) the critical need for prevention and planning, and (2) the essential importance of organisational preparedness.

The need for prevention and planning

Whenever a news organisation sends its journalists, or commissions a journalist, to enter an area of conflict, both the organisation and the individual have the duty to undertake steps to prevent kidnappings from happening. This requires effective threat assessments and ensuring proper training prior to deployment, and continuing communication and discussion of plans for coverage, travels, and meetings with parties to the conflict as journalists work in the field. It also requires that both be willing to say 'stop' when risk levels increase to unsuitable levels.

When they work in hostile environments, journalists are advised to keep editors and trusted local colleagues informed of their plans, hold discussions about how to interpret lapses in contact, and provide lists of people to be contacted in case they go missing.[4]

Because of the ubiquity of digital media that can be used against them, journalists working in potentially hostile environments need to be aware of their own social media footprint, ensuring that they do not compromise their own safety or that of colleagues. Information in social media becomes a weapon for captors during kidnapping. As the CPJ has noted:

> If you're taken captive, one of the first things a kidnapper may do is research your name on the Internet. Everything about you online will be seen by your abductors: where you have worked, the stories you have

reported, your education, your personal and professional associations, and possibly the value of your home and your family's net worth. You may want to limit the personal details or political leanings you reveal in your online profile. Be prepared to answer tough questions about your family, finances, reporting, and political associations.[5]

Journalists in conflict areas should also sanitise their equipment, carry a spare phone, ensure geolocators are removed if warranted, and be careful with what images they have publicly accessible of family/contacts on social media, being always aware that these can be used against them. It is important to ensure that their public profiles in social and other media do not compromise professional status or lead captors to suspect they are other than journalists. All of this requires a degree of individual responsibility, as does ensuring that they have appropriate training, equipment, risk assessments, personal insurance, communications plans, and leaving a document with colleagues giving details of the people they wish to be treated as next of kin in the event of an incident that compromises their safety. This should be updated regularly, because the designated person may change. In the event of a journalist being deployed to an area where kidnap is a threat, information that can help establish proof of life should also be included, such as several answers to questions that only the journalist (and certainly not the hostage taker) might know, although care should be taken with regard to how these questions and their answers can sometimes be misinterpreted.

Organisational preparedness is essential

News organisations sending journalists to or working with journalists in conflict zones need clear contingency plans for kidnappings. These include having relations with security firms in place to provide effective threat assessments and the ability to activate them as recovery specialists if needed, and taking out kidnapping insurance where warranted.

Clear company guidelines about what to do in the event of a kidnapping and who will be tasked to do it should be in place and ready for immediate implementation. A primary responsibility of organisations faced with the kidnapping of journalists working on their behalf is one of effective crisis management. Although they do not wish to publicly admit it, many news organisations have found themselves caught without robust crisis management plans in place during kidnappings and have been forced to piece together plans under the stress and duress of the moment, which creates delays in responding that have the potential to further endanger the journalist involved.

Effective crisis management plans consider how the organisation will structure its response, the fundamental principles and strategies that will govern the response, and the steps the organisation will take in that response. Prior planning and having processes and contingency options in place help the firm respond decisively in the early stages of a kidnapping and reduce the likelihood that the news organisation will become paralysed.

As noted earlier, it is important to rapidly focus key intelligence gathering that supports crisis resolution by asking and getting answers to questions. Who is holding our people and why? Who has the leverage to resolve this? Can we confirm proof of life? If the organisational response is slowed by lack of prior planning, addressing these questions may get postponed and further complicate resolution of the abduction.

Organisational response will need sustained support

Three levels of activities need to be supported and sustained during a kidnapping – strategic, tactical, and operational – and news organisations must be prepared to sustain them for extended periods if necessary.

Strategic activities involve creating a clear organisational policy direction on the overall processes and responsibility for handling a kidnapping, responding to demands, determining the veracity of information and claims, and payments for information and ransom.

Tactical activities include fact-finding, speaking to people who may have information – journalists on the ground, local authorities, and other contacts – that may identify abductors and their location, provide communication links to perpetrators, or help in a resolution.

Operational activities include a range of activities such as liaison with families/relatives of the kidnapped, liaison with government and other national authorities where appropriate, internal and external press relations, and making sure an organisation's crisis response team is both sustainable over the long haul and not too big and unwieldy. A single person (allowing for the fact that if it extends beyond a certain period of time, this person may need to have a deputy) should be in charge, and there should be identification of relevant experts, that is, legal and safety people within the organisation.

An important element of organisational preparedness is how to handle communications about the abduction, particularly because of the abilities of other parties – colleagues, family, and even kidnappers and their supporters – to use social media in ways that may not match the organisation's objectives and may complicate efforts to free the journalist. The rise of social media means that robust internal and external communication policies need to be in place to ensure that information from the news organisation is managed so as to avoid incidents where staff who have not been nominated as the company's spokespeople reveal information on their Twitter, Facebook, or other accounts that can endanger the journalist or send confused signals to the captors.

No news enterprise or journalist can ever be fully prepared for the personal, financial, and organisational toll created by a kidnapping. Understanding the phenomenon and preparing for the possibility, however, can help reduce the risks of kidnapping and speed and smooth a news organisation's response should one occur.

No publication can fully capture the extent of those factors or provide a complete understanding of everything that is encountered in responding to, or living through, a kidnapping. This publication has tried, however, to convey the kinds of issues and challenges the news industry faces because of kidnappings and to provide some basic advice and good practices when considering and preparing for the possibility.

Attacks on journalists, kidnapping, and deaths of journalists are deplorable, but would not occur unless the perpetrators believed that journalism and journalists were meaningful and important. The fact that journalists are willing to enter conflict zones to cover developments, that they will risk captivity to convey what is happening to the people of a country or region, and that they jeopardise their lives to reveal secrets and hold power to account are compelling testaments to the importance of news and information in society and the sacrifices that some make in pursuing the objective of an informed and knowledgeable public.

Journalism matters, but so do the lives of journalists. It behoves everyone in the news business to do all that can be done to provide the greatest possible protection and support for all journalists covering areas of conflict and high risk. Every journalist should understand and ameliorate the risks incurred in carrying out their professional missions.

Journalism is not an innocuous and risk-free activity and none of us would want it to be so bland, inoffensive, and uninformed that it would become so. Nevertheless, we must find ways to improve the safety of our colleagues in the field and to bring to justice those who hold them hostage and deliberately injure or kill them with impunity.

Appendix 1: Safety Training and Learning Resources

Columbia University School of Journalism, Reporting Safely in Crisis Zones Workshop, http://dartcenter.org/media/reporting-safely-crisis-zones-course.

Committee to Protect Journalists, Journalist Security Guide, https://www.cpj.org/reports/2012/04/journalist-security-guide.php.

Dart Center for Journalism & Trauma, tip sheets and guides, http://dartcenter.org.

Global Journalist Security, https://www.journalistsecurity.net/2012/11/30/personal-safety-classes-in-2013.

International Center for Journalists, training manuals, http://www.icfj.org/Resources/tabid/209/Default.aspx.

International Federation of Journalists, Live News Survival Guide, http://www.ifj.org/nc/news-single-view/backpid/59/article/ifj-live-news-survival-guide-for-journalists/.

International News Safety Institute, Training, http://www.newssafety.org/safety/training.

Institute of War and Peace Reporting, Training Manual, https://iwpr.net/printed-materials/reporting-change-handbook.

Reporters Sans Frontières, Handbook for Journalists, http://en.rsf.org/handbook-for-journalists-january-17-04-2007,21744.html.

Appendix 2: Crisis Support Organisations and Resources for Journalists and their Families

Committee to Protect Journalists, https://cpj.org/campaigns/assistance/what-we-do.php.

Federal Bureau of Investigation, Coping after Terrorism for Survivors, https://www.fbi.gov/stats-services/victim_assistance/cope_terror.

Hostage UK, http://www.hostageuk.org/.

International News Safety Institute, Response 24, http://www.newssafety.org/safety/response24/.

Reporters Sans Frontières, http://en.rsf.org/supporting-an-protecting-12-09-2012,43368.html.

Web MD, Post-Traumatic Stress Disorder, http://www.webmd.com/mental-health/tc/post-traumatic-stress-disorder--topic-overview.

Appendix 3: Selected Providers of Insurance and Consultancy

Selected providers of kidnapping, ransom, and extortion insurance

AIG (global insurance firm based in the US), http://www.aig.com/Kidnap-Ransom-and-Extortion-KRE-Liability_3171_417761.html.

Aon (global risk management, insurance and reinsurance brokerage), http://www.aon.com/risk-services/crisis-management/kidnap-ransom.jsp.

Aspen APJ (asset protection underwriter based in Jersey), http://www.aspen-apj.com/en/.

Chubb Insurance of Europe (global insurance firm), http://www.chubb.com/international/uk/csi/chubb9331.html.

Clements Worldwide (global insurance firm based in the US), https://www.clements.com/intl-specialty-commercial/kidnap-ransom.

HCC Insurance (US-based specialty insurance firm), http://www.hcc.com.

Hiscox (Lloyds of London underwriter based in Bermuda), http://www.hiscoxbroker.com/other-commercial-insurance/kidnap-and-ransom/.

Petersen International Underwriters (Lloyd's coverholder based in US), https://www.piu.org/contingent-insurance.

Travelers (global insurance firm based in the US), https://www.travelers.com/business-insurance/management-professional-liability/private-non-profit/kidnap-ransom.aspx.

XL Caitlin (global insurance and reinsurance firm and Lloyds underwriter), http://www.catlin.com/en/asiapacific/insurance/war-political-risk/kidnap-ransom.

Selected providers of security and recovery consultancy services

AKE Group (UK-based global risk mitigation firm), http://www.akegroup.com.

Marsh (global risk assessment and solution firm), https://www.marsh.com.

Olive Group (global risk, security and crisis services firm), http://www.olivegroup.com.

Special Contingency Risks (UK-based crisis and risk mitigation and crisis management firm), https://www.scr-ltd.co.uk/#&panel1-1.

Steve Vickers and Associates (Hong Kong-based risked and security consulting firm), http://stevevickersassociates.com.

Terra Firma Risk Management (UK-based risk management and crisis consultancy), http://www.terrafirma-rm.com.

Willis (global security solutions firm), http://www.willis.com.

Notes

Chapter 1   Journalists are Vulnerable Targets

1 Reporters Sans Frontières, 'Roundup of Abuses Against Journalists, 2014', http://rsf.org/files/bilan-2014-EN.pdf#page=1.

2 http://www.newssafety.org/underthreat/#. In the interest of transparency, one of the authors of this book – Hannah Storm – is employed by the International News Safety Institute. The authors have endeavoured to ensure that the INSI is not given undue prominence in the study compared to other journalistic organisations that also play crucial roles in promoting safety and protecting journalists.

3 International News Safety Institute, *Under Threat: The Changing State of Media Safety*, http://www.newssafety.org/underthreat/under-threat-the-findings.html#Bombs _Bullets_and_Kidnapping.

4 UN Security Council, Resolution 2222 (2015), adopted by the Security Council at its 7450th meeting, on 27 May 2015, http://www.un.org/en/ga/search/view_doc.asp? symbol=S/RES/2222%282015%29.

5 World Association of Newspaper and News Publishers, 'World's Press Calls for Greater Protection of Journalists', press release, 31 May 2015.

6 UNESCO, Safety of Journalists and Impunity, http://www.unesco.org/new/en/ communication-and-information/freedom-of-expression/safety-of-journalists/ #sthash.aPCNhvDQ.dpuf.

7 Reporters Sans Frontières, 'UN General Assembly Adopts Resolution on Journalists' Safety', 26 Nov. 2013, http://en.rsf.org/un-general-assembly-adopts-26-11-2013,45512.html.

8 Interview, 3 Sept. 2014.

9 Marisol Bello, 'Kidnapping Westerners is Big Business', *USA Today*, 21 Aug. 2014, http://www.usatoday.com/story/news/world/2014/08/20/james-foley-islamic-state-kidnapping/14350483.

10 David Abel and John R. Ellement, 'Freed Journalist Thanks All Who Fought for him', *Boston Globe*, 28 Aug. 2014, B1.

11 'Journalists as Spies', *Editor and Publisher*, 129/32 (10 Aug. 1996).

12 http://www.bbc.com/news/uk-21628728.

13 Mariah Blake, 'German "CIA" Used Reporters as Informants', *Christian Science Monitor*, 18 May 2006, http://www.csmonitor.com/2006/0518/p06s02-woeu.html.

14 http://www.ottawamagazine.com/society/2012/09/22/the-ex-files-journalist-mark-bourries-behind-the-scenes-account-of-his-two-years-in-the-employ-of-xinhua.

15 'Spies and Journalists: Taking a Look at their Intersections', *Nieman Reports*, Fall 2009; Stephen Dorril, 'Russia Accuses Fleet Street: Journalists and MI6 during the Cold War', *International Journal of Press/Politics*, 20/3 (2015), 204–27.

Chapter 2   Relations with Governments during Kidnappings

1 Rukmini Callimachi, 'Paying Ransoms, Europe Bankrolls Qaeda Terror', *New York Times*, 29 July 2014, http://www.nytimes.com/2014/07/30/world/africa/ransoming-citizens-europe-becomes-al-qaedas-patron.html?_r=0.

2 David Blair, 'Should Governments Pay Ransom for Hostages?', *Telegraph*, 21 Aug. 2014, http://www.telegraph.co.uk/news/worldnews/11048734/Should-governments-pay-a-ransom-for-hostages.html.

3 United Nations Security Council Resolution 2133, 27 Jan. 2014, http://unscr.com/en/resolutions/2133.

4 http://edition.cnn.com/2014/08/22/opinion/bergen-schneider-isis-ransom.

5 http://www.thetimes.co.uk/tto/news/world/europe/article4292595.ece.

6 http://blogs.reuters.com/david-rohde/2014/08/20/did-american-policy-help-kill-james-foley.

7 http://www.bbc.co.uk/news/world-middle-east-28875926.

8 http://www.nytimes.com/2014/07/30/world/africa/ransoming-citizens-europe-becomes-al-qaedas-patron.html.

9 Rukmini Callimachi, 'Paying Ransoms, Europe Bankrolls Qaeda Terror', *New York Times*, 29 July 2014, http://www.nytimes.com/2014/07/30/world/africa/ransoming-citizens-europe-becomes-al-qaedas-patron.html?_r=0; Peter Bergen and Emily Schneider, 'Should Nations Just Pay ISIS Ransom?', CNN, 22 Jan. 2015, http://www.cnn.com/2015/01/20/opinion/bergen-schneider-isis-ransom-new/index.html.

10 David Cohen, 'Why the U.S. Does Not Pay Ransoms for Americans Kidnapped by Terrorists', *Newsweek*, 23 Aug. 2014, http://www.newsweek.com/why-us-does-not-pay-ransoms-americans-kidnapped-terrorists-266315; Ian Black and Julian Berger, 'British Government Faces Dilemma by Refusing to Pay Hostage Ransoms to Isis', *Guardian*, 2 Sept. 2014, http://www.theguardian.com/world/2014/sep/02/british-government-dilemma-refusing-pay-hostage-ransom-isis.

11 http://abcnews.go.com/International/government-threatened-foley-family-ransom-payments-mother-slain/story?id=25453963.

12 Julie Pace and Eric Tucker, 'US Won't Prosecute Hostages' Families Who Pay Ransom', Associated Press, 23 June 2015, http://news.yahoo.com/us-wont-prosecute-hostages-families-pay-ransom-172301570.html#.

13 The White House, 'Fact Sheet: US Government Hostage Policy', 24 June 2015, https://www.whitehouse.gov/the-press-office/2015/06/24/fact-sheet-us-government-hostage-policy.

14 http://www.telegraph.co.uk/news/worldnews/islamic-state/11254950/Counter-terrorism-Bill-What-it-contains.html.

15 Shane Croucher, 'Isis: Why Theresa May's Ban on UK Insurers Paying Ransom Claims Changes Little', 24 Nov. 2014, www.ibtimes.co.uk/isis-why-theresa-mays-ban-uk-insurers-paying-ransom-claims-changes-little-1476341.

16 http://www.bbc.co.uk/news/uk-30440742.

17 http://edition.cnn.com/2014/12/06/world/meast/yemen-u-s-hostage-killed.

18 http://www.independent.co.uk/news/world/middle-east/pierre-korkie-and-luke-somers-killings-analysis-more-failures-than-successes-in-hostage-rescue-attempts-9909249.html.

Chapter 3   Organisational Responses to Kidnappings

1 Interview with K&R expert who wished to remain anonymous, Jan. 2015.

2 Interview, 3 Sept. 2014.

3 INSI, *Under Threat*.

4 Peter Apps, 'Kidnap and Ransom: Negotiating Lives for Cash', Reuters, 17 Feb. 2011, http://www.reuters.com/article/2011/02/17/us-crime-kidnap-ransom-idUSTRE71G3U520110217.

5 Julian Borger, Kim Willsher, and Stephen Burgen, 'Terrorist Ransoms: Should Governments Pay up or Stick to their Principles', *Guardian*, 22 Aug. 2014, http://www.theguardian.com/media/2014/aug/22/terrorist-ransom-government-pay-james-foley.

6 Nicholas Watt and Alan Travis, 'Anti-Terrorism Measure: May Aims to Close Ransom Loophole', *Guardian*, 14 Nov. 2014, http://www.theguardian.com/politics/2014/nov/24/ransom-payments-isis-anti-terrorism-amendment-law-theresa-may.

Chapter 4   Experiencing Kidnapping

1 David Rohde, '7 Months, 10 Days in Captivity', *New York Times*, 17 Oct. 2009, http://www.nytimes.com/2009/10/18/world/asia/18hostage.html?pagewanted=all&_r=0.

Chapter 5   Coverage of Journalist Kidnappings

1 Rob C. Mawby, 'Visibility, Transparency and Police–Media Relations', *Policing and Society*, 9/3 (1999), 263–86.

2 Garth Crandon, *The Police and the Media: Information Management and the Construction of Crime News* (Bradford: Horton Publishing, 1992); Steven Chermak, 'Image Control: How Police Affect the Presentation of Crime News', *American Journal of Police*, 14/2 (1995), 21–43; Steven Chermak and Alexander Weiss, 'Maintaining Legitimacy Using External Communication Strategies: An Analysis of Police–Media Relations', *Journal of Criminal Justice*, 33/5 (2005), 501–12.

3 Michael T. McEwen and Stephen Sloan, 'Terrorism: Police and Press Problems', *Terrorism*, 2/1–2 (1979), 1–54; Robert G. Picard, *Media Portrayals of Terrorism:*

Functions and Meanings of News Coverage (Ames, IA: Iowa State University Press, 1993).

4   Jennifer Shaw et al., *Kidnapping, Terrorism and the News Media in Britain* (London: Royal United Services Institute for Defence Studies, 1979); M. Cherif Bassiouni, 'Terrorism, Law Enforcement, and the Mass Media: Perspectives, Problems, Proposals', *Journal of Criminal Law and Criminology*, 72/1 (1981), 1–51.

5   Agence France-Presse, 'French TV, Radio Stations Rapped for Charlie Hebdo Attacks Coverage', *Japan Times*, 13 Feb. 2015, http://www.japantimes.co.jp/news/2015/02/13/world/french-tv-radio-stations-rapped-charlie-hebdo-attacks-coverage/#.VZkyrPlUGUl; 'Paris Supermarket Siege Survivors Sue Media over "Dangerous" Coverage', *Guardian*, 3 Apr. 2015, http://www.theguardian.com/world/2015/apr/03/paris-supermarket-siege-survivors-sue-media.

6   R. Scanlin, 'Coping with the Media: Police–Media Problems and Tactics in Hostage Takings and Terrorist Incidents', *Canadian Police College Journal*, 5/3 (1981), 129–48.

7   Raphael Cohen-Almagor, 'Media Coverage of Acts of Terrorism: Troubling Episodes and Suggested Guidelines', *Canadian Journal of Communication*, 30 (Sept. 2005), http://cjc-online.ca/index.php/journal/article/view/1579.

8   The BBC has editorial guidelines governing coverage of war, terror, and emergencies including hijacking, kidnapping, hostage taking and sieges, and bombing. See BBC Editorial Guidelines, 1 June 2014.

9   'Kidnapped Journalist in Brazil TV Plea', Al Jazeera, 13 Aug. 2006, http://www.aljazeera.com/archive/2006/08/20084915249924263.html.

10   See, for example, J. Katz, 'What Makes Crime "News"', *Media, Culture and Society*, 9/1 (1987), 47–75; David Pritchard and Karen Hughes, 'Patterns of Deviance in Crime News', *Journal of Communication*, 47/3 (1997), 49–67; Eileen Bjornstrom, Robert Kaufman, Ruth Peterson, and Michael Slater, 'Race and Ethnic Representations of Lawbreakers and Victims in Crime News: A National Study of Television Coverage', *Social Problems*, 57/2 (May 2010), 269–93; Travis Dixon and Charlotte Williams, 'The Changing Misrepresentation of Race and Crime on Network and Cable News', *Journal of Communication*, 65/1 (2014), 24; Jeff Gruenewald, Steven Chermak, and Jesenia Pizarro, 'Covering Victims in the News: What Makes Minority Homicides Newsworthy?', *Justice Quarterly*, 30/5 (2013), 755–83.

11   Society of Professional Journalists, Code of Ethics, http://www.spj.org/ethicscode.asp.

12   See, for example, M. L. Stein, 'Media Keeps Lid on Kidnapping', *Editor & Publisher*, 130/5 (1 Feb. 1997), about a child's kidnapping which the media voluntarily did not cover at the request of the police.

13   See, for example, Barbara J. Wilson, Nicole Martins, and Amy L. Marske, 'Children's and Parents' Fright Reactions to Kidnapping Stories in the News', *Communication Monographs*, 72/1 (2005), 46–70, and Pamela Anne Quiroz and Nilda Flores-González, 'Crime, News and Fear of Crime: Toward an Identification of Audience Effect', *Social Problems*, 44/3 (1997), 342–57.

14   Robert G. Picard, 'Journalists as Targets and Victims of Terrorism', in Yonah Alexander and Robert G. Picard (eds), *In the Camera's Eye: News Coverage of Terrorist Events* (Washington, DC: Macmillan-Brassey's, 1991); A. Odasuo Alali

and Kenoye Kelvin Eke (eds), *Media Coverage of Terrorism* (Newbury Park, CA: Sage Publications, 1991).

15 Picard, *Media Portrayals of Terrorism*; Alexander and Picard, *In the Camera's Eye*.

16 Picard, *Media Portrayals of Terrorism*; Pippa Norris, Montague Kern, and Marion Just (eds), *Framing Terrorism: The News Media, the Government and the Public* (New York: Routledge, 2003).

17 Phillip Seib, *Global Terrorism and New Media: The Post-Al Qaeda Generation* (New York: Routledge, 2010).

18 Peter Gelling, 'US Journalist Missing in Syria', 2 Jan. 2013, http://www.globalpost.com/dispatch/news/regions/middle-east/syria/121127/kidnapped-journalists-syria-american-james-foley-richard-engel-nbc-austin-tice.

19 Keren Tenenboim-Weinblatt, 'The Management of Visibility: Media Coverage of Kidnapping and Captivity Cases around the World', *Media, Culture and Society*, 35/7 (2013), 791–808.

20 Interview, 3 Sept. 2014.

21 Rukmini Callimachi and Elaine Ganley, 'Officials: Two French Journalists Killed in Mali', *USA Today*, 3 Nov. 2013, http://www.usatoday.com/story/news/world/2013/11/02/french-say-2-journalists-killed-in-north-mali/3385277.

22 BBC News, 'Two French Journalists Killed in Mali Town of Kidal', 2 Nov. 2013, http://www.bbc.com/news/world-africa-24787682.

23 Ashley Fantz and Paul Vercammen, 'American Journalist Freed from Somali Pirates', 24 Sept. 2014, http://www.cnn.com/2014/09/23/world/africa/somalia-american-journalist-released/index.html.

24 Rem Reider, 'For NBC Another Fiasco to Explain', *USA Today*, 17 Apr. 2015, 2B.

25 Julia Angwin, 'Should Journalists in War Zones Carry Weapons?', *Wall Street Journal*, 29 Dec. 2003, http://www.wsj.com/articles/SB107266320854789600.

26 Kelly Heyboer, 'Guns Under Fire', *American Journalism Review* (Apr./May 2014), http://ajrarchive.org/Article.asp?id=3651.

27 Sherry Ricchiardi, 'Gun-Toting Journalists', *American Journalism Review* (Oct./Nov. 2005), http://ajrarchive.org/Article.asp?id=3969; Radio Free Europe/Radio Liberty, 'Pakistani Journalists Allowed to Carry Weapons', 1 June 2011, http://www.rferl.org/content/pakistan_journalists_allowed_carry_weapons/24212138.html.

28 CBC Guidelines on Covering Kidnapping and Hostage Situations, 7 Oct. 2009, http://www.caj.ca/wp-content/uploads/2009/11/CBC-Guidelines-on-Covering-Kidnapping-and-Hostage-Situations-_-The-National.pdf.

29 Joel Simon, 'Is it Time to End Media Blackouts?', *Columbia Journalism Review*, 3 Sept. 2014, http://www.cjr.org/the_kicker/james_foley_steven_sotloff_media_blackout.php; On the Media, 'Transcript: Not Reporting Journalist Kidnappings', 5 Sept. 2014, http://www.onthemedia.org/story/not-reporting-journalist-kidnappings/transcript; National Public Radio, 'Reporter's Escape from Taliban Spurs Ethics Debate', http://www.npr.org/templates/story/story.php?storyId=105775059; John Cook, 'Fifteen Ways of Looking at the Media Blackout of Richard Engel's Abduction, Vol. II: Against', Gawker, http://gawker.com/5969866/fifteen-ways-of-looking-at-the-media-blackout-of-richard-engels-abduction-vol-ii-against; Frank Smyth, 'Do News Blackouts Help Journalists Held Captive?', Committee to Protect Journalists, https://cpj.org/blog/2013/02/do-news-blackouts-help-journalists-held-captive.php;

Frank Smyth, 'When Journalists are Captured, is Silence or Publicity the Best Policy?', Huffington Post, http://www.huffingtonpost.com/committee-to-protect-journalists/when-journalists-are-capt_b_2783795.html.

30 David Rohde, 'An Epidemic of Journalist Kidnappings in Syria', *The Atlantic*, 18 Nov. 2013, http://www.theatlantic.com/international/archive/2013/11/an-epidemic-of-journalist-kidnappings-in-syria/281574.

Chapter 6   The Roles of Journalist Safety Organisations

1 'WAN-IFRA Appalled by Gruesome Murder of War Correspondent Steven Sotloff', http://blog.wan-ifra.org/2014/09/03/wan-ifra-appalled-by-gruesome-murder-of-war-correspondent-steven-sotloff.

2 Sherry Ricchiard, 'Global Coalition Sets Safety Standards for Freelance Journalists', International Center for Journalists, 25 Feb. 2015, http://ijnet.org/en/blog/global-coalition-sets-safety-standards-freelance-journalists.

3 Video statement by Joel Simon, https://www.cpj.org/about/ from approx. 03:26.

4 Email to the authors, June 2015.

5 Email to the authors, June 2015.

6 Email to the authors, 10 July 2015.

7 PBS News Hour, 'Report: Female Journalists Facing More Risks, Intimidation Abroad', 4 July 2011, http://www.pbs.org/newshour/bb/media-july-dec11-journalists_07-04.

8 Email to the authors, June 2015.

9 Email to the authors, June 2015.

10 http://www.newssafety.org/underthreat/under-threat-the-findings.html#Training_and_Equipment.

11 http://www.newssafety.org/underthreat/under-threat-the-findings.html#Training_and_Equipment.

12 http://www.cjr.org/the_kicker/james_foley_steven_sotloff_media_blackout.php.

13 Email to the authors, June 2015.

14 Email to the authors, 10 July 2015.

15 Telephone interview with the authors, Mar. 2015.

16 Email to the authors, July 2015.

Chapter 7   Good Practices for Journalists and their Employers

1 INSN, *Under Threat.*

2 Ibid.

3 Ibid.

4 CPJ Journalist's Security Guide, 'Captive Situations', http://www.cpj.org/reports/2012/04/journalist-security-guide.php.

5 Ibid.

Media, Revolution and Politics in Egypt: The Story of an Uprising
Abdalla F. Hassan
ISBN: 978 1 78453 217 8 (HB); 978 1 78453 218 5 (PB)

The Euro Crisis in the Media: Journalistic Coverage of Economic Crisis and European Institutions
Robert G. Picard (ed.)
ISBN: 978 1 78453 059 4 (HB); 978 1 78453 060 0 (PB)

Local Journalism: The Decline of Newspapers and the Rise of Digital Media
Rasmus Kleis Nielsen (ed.)
ISBN: 978 1 78453 320 5 (HB); 978 1 78453 321 2 (PB)

The Ethics of Journalism: Individual, Institutional and Cultural Influences
Wendy N. Wyatt (ed.)
ISBN: 978 1 78076 673 7 (HB); 978 1 78076 674 4 (PB)

Political Journalism in Transition: Western Europe in a Comparative Perspective
Raymond Kuhn and Rasmus Kleis Nielsen (eds)
ISBN: 978 1 78076 677 5 (HB); 978 1 78076 678 2 (PB)

Transparency in Politics and the Media: Accountability and Open Government
Nigel Bowles, James T. Hamilton and David A. L. Levy (eds)
ISBN: 978 1 78076 675 1 (HB); 978 1 78076 676 8 (PB)

Media and Public Shaming: Drawing the Boundaries of Disclosure
Julian Petley (ed.)
ISBN: 978 1 78076 586 0 (HB); 978 1 78076 587 7 (PB)